"Bear is a man's man (check out his name!) in the best sense. Strength, courage, virtue—all brought to perfection by the true man, Jesus Christ—Bear brings to Christian men, who are often unsure about what a true man is supposed to be. *Deep Adventure* surfs men through culture's treacherous moral waters to their final home on the shore, for their sake and for the sake of those they love."

—DR. RAY GUARENDI, nationally syndicated radio and television host and bestselling author

"The effeminization of men is rampant in our culture. This book counters that; it is muscular Christianity, it is like a piece of 'red meat' for Catholic men. Bear Woznick provides the encouragement and the tools in this book so that men can 'stand in the breach' (Ezekiel 22:30) and make a difference in the public square. This book is vintage New Evangelization, it will inspire and empower Catholic men to know, live, and spread their faith."

—JESSE ROMERO, Catholic evangelist and author, *Catholics, Wake Up!*

"You've never read a book like this before. You're going to love it. And you're going to love what it does to your life—though you might find the demands daunting and difficult. God made you to be a hero, and Bear is ready to train you for the heroic tasks ahead. Get ready to ride some mighty waves."

—MIKE AQUILINA, EWTN host and author, *Angels of God*

"I've never surfed, ridden a Harley, scuba dived, or skydived. But I can affirm wholeheartedly with Bear the deep conviction that is at the heart of his book: 'The most radical thing that you can do in life is to abandon yourself to the wild adventure of God's will.'"

—BISHOP MICHAEL BYRNES, auxiliary bishop of the Archdiocese of Detroit

"Take the spiritual classics of the desert fathers, put them in the hands of a modern ocean master and champion surfer, reintroduce them to modern culture with lost words like heroism and virtue, and the misunderstood concept of manliness, and you have this powerful blast of clarity and pull of gravity toward the greatest force of nature: God who is love. Women, encourage men to take up this adventure. Put this book in their hands, and challenge them to go deeper into the discovery of a force more powerful than they can know without it."

—SHEILA LIAUGMINAS, EWTN radio host
and author, *Non-Negotiable*

"Men need examples—heroic role models they can look up to. Unhappily, heroes are rare today. That's where Bear comes in. He is a manly man who has proved his moral courage and manly example in many ways, in the world of sports, everyday life, and ideas. The title of Bear's new book is a dead giveaway. *Deep Adventure* prepares you for a plunge into a life of excitement and challenge. Get this into the hands of the men in your life and give them an example of manly and heroic living."

—STEVE RAY, author, movie producer, and pilgrimage leader

"Bear Woznick—surfer, pilot, black-belt, and adventurer—is such a strong Christian man of God, his readers truly want to become heroic in their pursuit and performance of the Christian virtues. His latest book is fun, intelligent, confident, and fiercely faithful—just like the author."

—ANTHONY DESTEFANO, bestselling author,
A Travel Guide to Heaven

DEEP ADVENTURE
The Way of Heroic Virtue

Bear Woznick

servant
AN IMPRINT OF
FRANCISCAN MEDIA
Cincinnati, Ohio

Cover and book design by Mark Sullivan
Cover image © David Pu'u • www.davidpuu.com

LIBRARY OF CONGRESS CATALOGING-IN-PUBLICATION DATA
Names: Woznick, Bear, author.
Title: Deep adventure : the way of heroic virtue / Bear Woznick.
Description: Cincinnati : Servant, 2016. | Includes bibliographical references and index.
Identifiers: LCCN 2016004553 | ISBN 9781632530288 (pbk. : alk. paper)
Subjects: LCSH: Courage—Religious aspects—Christianity. | Heroes—Religious
aspects—Christianity. | Heroic virtue. | Virtues. | Christian ethics—Catholic authors.
Classification: LCC BV4647.C75 W69 2016 | DDC 248.4—dc23
LC record available at http://lccn.loc.gov/2016004553

ISBN 978-1-63253-028-8

Published by Servant
an imprint of Franciscan Media
28 W. Liberty St.
Cincinnati, OH 45202
www.FranciscanMedia.org

Printed in the United States of America.
Printed on acid-free paper.
16 17 18 19 20 5 4 3 2 1

This book is dedicated to all of the faithful listeners of *Deep Adventure Radio* and the partners of Deep Adventure Ministries.

I also want to dedicate this book to Mother Angelica, whose bold faith to follow the leading of the Holy Spirit and whose diligent faithfulness to solid teaching through EWTN revived and empowered me. I want to dedicate this to everyone involved at every level and in any way with EWTN for their hard work and their support.

CONTENTS

I want to thank everyone who believed in this project and stood by me in my efforts. My father, Deacon Greg Woznick, who called me often to encourage me as well as to tell me another joke. To my mother, Mereece. When she went to heaven, I experienced an immediate explosion of grace in my life, and I know she prays for me. Thanks, Mom.

To my friends and family, who encouraged me as I hid away in my Bear's den to write, and to my fellow surfers, who never seemed to mind that I wasn't taking up space in the lineup.

I want to thank Lindsay Olson, who mercilessly brandished the editor's sword in keeping me from going down too many rabbit holes. It goes without saying to thank Ron Burgandy for his constant help, insight, inspiration, and ability to stay classy.

I want to thank all those who believe in and support Deep Adventure Ministries.

May the Breath of the Holy Spirit Aloha you.

I gaze out my window over the south shore of Waikiki. Cooling trade winds blow through the windows on the maukau *(mountain) side of my home to the* makai *(ocean) side, where I stand drinking my third cup of rich Kona coffee. Multiple rainbows glisten over the volcanic ridge line of the Ko'olaus. The lightest spritzing of mist drifts in with the bright sunshine and kisses my skin with the cooling "blessing," which is what we call rain in Hawaii.*

All morning, I have been distracted from my work, glancing up repeatedly to witness this new south swell. The waves are constantly growing, bumping up in size by more than two feet an hour. A friend of mine and wave forecaster, Gary Kewley, who runs SurfNewsNetwork.com, predicted this would be the biggest swell of the summer season so far, and he is right. I know that the surf cam in my window is live streaming the event of the year online to several thousand people an hour. The coconut telegraph will be going off with surfers connecting with each other to jam down to the beach to surf, calling their employers with a myriad of excuses to be late.

I see the lines of a monster set forming on the horizon. I stand at reverent attention, grabbing my binoculars and looking out past what we surfers call Fours, my favorite spot. Fours only breaks when the swell starts to get big, and it was ready to fire.

I know this set will put the dive boats, which bring island visitors out to snorkel, in jeopardy of being pitchpoled. If the captains aren't prudent, it will mean a long day of ocean rescues for lifeguards. For surfers, though, it is going to be a good day. I watch as the waves peak about a half mile from shore. The trade winds blow out to sea toward them. The fifteen-knot winds hold the waves upright and feather their lips backward, but fortunately the crests of the waves do not break until they roll under and past the boats, finally launching into hollow, barreling waves just a few yards past them.

I have seen enough. Work can wait, but the waves will not. I grab my seven-foot-long carbon fiber stand-up paddle. I want to stand-up paddle if I can because there is nothing quite like the feeling of acceleration as you free-fall into a fifteen-foot face when you are starting from a standing position. Besides, by standing I can see the next wave sooner and gauge where to paddle in order to catch it.

I look out my window one more time. The boat captains have called in the snorkelers and are pulling anchor to head for the safety of their port. Dozens of surfers start making their way back to the safer inside breaks. Only a few adventure-seeking surfers paddle out.

The

Way

of

Heroic

Virtue

CHAPTER ONE
THE CALL TO HEROIC VIRTUE

My son, Shane, and I were standing in front of my home on the sands of Waikiki, when suddenly he sprinted toward the rocky jetty that points like a fist out to the sea. He ran waist-deep into the waves, racing for a young woman whose surfboard was rocketing toward the jagged rocks.

She screamed and Shane leaped forward. He scooped her up in his powerful arms and rolled, letting his momentum carry them both off the other side of the board. He enveloped her protectively and put his body between hers and the treacherous rocks as the wave hurtled them against the sharp face of the boulders. When the wave flooded back out to sea, it sent her surfboard—still attached to her ankle by the leg leash—careening toward them with the ferocity of an angry shark. Shane held her close to his chest with one arm and unhooked her leg leash with the other. When he made a run for it, the riptide slammed the board against his shins, gashing them. He pushed past it and brought her safely to higher ground.

He set her down by the lifeguard tower, and she began inspecting her body for broken bones or lacerations before realizing that he had protected her from the worst of it. They were both bloody, but it was mostly Shane's blood staining their skin. She had only one small cut. Even as the lifeguards carried her away, the girl never took her eyes off Shane. Her gaze shone with gratitude.

Shane walked the way of heroic virtue.

Our culture has a very confused sense of heroism, often applauding the biggest, strongest, loudest, or wealthiest. Blockbuster movies and an endless parade of celebrities and sports figures dominate the mainstream representation of heroes. But true heroism—the kind that saves lives, preserves dignity, and protects the most vulnerable—is a determined, steadfast power, under control and directed toward the good with the clarity of purpose that comes with humility. A hero isn't someone born with unconquerable strength and selflessness. Heroes are not formed in a cataclysmic instant. Heroism is developed over time, one decision after another, moment by moment, formed by a deliberate, chosen, and habitual response to life.

A hero is cultivated by countless—often unnoticed—actions. Heroes are not made by a spider's bite or on an alien planet. They are ordinary humans—you and me—who direct their decisions and actions to be strengthened by goodness, compassion, integrity, and righteousness. They are the ones who are willing to venture out of the safe harbor of what is comfortable and venture into the wild, untamable sea of God's calling. In other words, the hero's journey is one of deep virtue.

There are two types of virtues proposed by the Catholic Church: the cardinal virtues and the theological virtues. The cardinal virtues—also called the moral, human, or natural virtues—are justice, temperance, prudence, and fortitude. The three theological virtues—also called the spiritual or Godward virtues—as described by Paul, are faith, hope, and love.

Each virtue plays an important role in our relationship with God and others, and each calls us deeper into the wave of God's unexpected adventure for our lives. By choosing to live virtuously, by intentionally seeking to develop the seven virtues in our lives and hearts, we are choosing to immerse ourselves in God's will. In this book, I will explore the seven virtues, demonstrating how they equip all of us to walk in the way of the hero and enable us to venture more deeply into the dynamic love of God.

Around the year 500 BC, the Greek philosopher Socrates declared that the habitual practice of the four moral virtues of justice, prudence, temperance, and fortitude was the only path to happiness. His teaching contradicted the Greek belief and practice of appeasing the melodramatic pantheon of gods. To the contrary, he reasoned that there could be only one true God. He believed that "no evil can befall a good man." Evil can assault a man in many ways, but it can never harm the soul of a good man since he would only grow in virtue as a result. However, the evil man does harm to his own soul. Socrates held fast to his convictions and paid the ultimate price when he willingly died for embracing these virtues and for refusing to deny his reasoned belief in there being only one God. The ruling powers, irritated by his politics, philosophy, and religious beliefs, sentenced him to execution by poison. Socrates walked the way of heroic virtue.

The book of Wisdom says, "And if any one loves righteousness, her labors are virtues; for she teaches self-control and prudence, justice and courage; nothing in life is more profitable for men than these" (8:7). Socrates believed that if people truly understood that living the virtuous life was the key to happiness, then everyone would naturally live perfectly virtuous lives. But St. Paul had a different view on humanity's ability and willingness to do so. He knew that the human soul is wounded and has an inclination toward evil. He understood that we inherited a fallen nature.

St. Paul groaned in Romans 7:15, "I do not understand my own actions. For I do not do what I want, but I do the very thing I hate." He knew that man's will to pursue the moral virtues is weakened by original sin. Our fallen nature resists our pursuit of virtue. As Paul continues, "So then, brothers and sisters, we are debtors, not to the flesh, to live according to the flesh—for if you live according to the flesh, you will die; but if by the Spirit you put to death the deeds of the body, you will live. For all who are led by the Spirit of God are children of God" (Romans 8:12–14).

I spend a lot of time in Cocoa Beach, Florida, and I often get to watch rocket launches. In these verses from Romans, Paul is saying that we cannot pull ourselves out of the deteriorating orbit of sin without a rocket engine—that is, the power of grace. Through the writings of St. Paul, God gives us the rocket ship we so desperately need. The theological virtues of faith and hope are the booster rockets, with love as the primary rocket.

Paul was no pseudo-spiritualist wimp or soft philosopher. His beliefs compelled him to venture forth into distant lands and hostile environments on his mission to spread the good news and rescue a dying world. He was like a real-life Rocky Balboa. Every time he was knocked down, he got back up and kept fighting. He was beaten with rods three times, pelted with stones and left for dead once, and shipwrecked three times (2 Corinthians 11:25). Yet, he spoke boldly of his faith and showed those around him the love of Christ. I have been in St. Paul's last prison cell outside of Rome, along the Appian Way. I have the seen the stone pillar where he placed his neck just before the executioner's sword swung down in a powerful, deadly arch. Whether in prison or free, hungry or feasting, alone or in a crowd, he fought the good fight; he finished the race (1 Timothy 6:12). Paul walked the way of the heroic virtue.

That fateful day on the beach, Shane demonstrated all of the virtues. We can see in his actions the four cardinal virtues. When he and I stood at the high tide mark, looking out to sea, we both followed the ancient surfer's adage, taught to me by my father: "Never turn your back on the ocean." Shane applied this wisdom to his life daily, and it was this prudence that kept him alert so he was aware of the young surfer's distress. His ongoing commitment to the virtue of self-mastery, or temperance, kept him clean, competent, and in good physical shape. Because of this, he was not only willing to respond to the emergency but was *able* to respond to it. Part of his role as a beach boy who rented boards out to beginners was to stay alert for any danger to the renters, whether they were on a board he'd rented or on someone else's. It is the beach boy code. In this manner, he exhibited the virtue of justice, by giving the surfer the protection she had due from him or any other beach boy. Finally, it was his developed virtue of fortitude that propelled him toward her, in spite of the danger to himself. His courage was demonstrated in his willingness to sacrifice himself and take the brunt of the damage.

We also see in his actions the three theological virtues. It was certainly faith and hope that propelled him into a selfless act of love to save her. He believed that God would help him as he ran to the rescue and hoped in God's protection as he leaped into the water. His actions were an act of self-donation and love.

Like the indomitable cowboys of the old western films, riding into town to save the day, these are the true magnificent seven virtues. For each hero, there is a point of departure from the norm. This is where the true adventure begins. A hero is just a common person, like you and me, choosing to do an uncommon thing. Virtue challenges us to lay down our life in service to God's perfect will. Long before believers were called Christians, their beliefs were referred to as The Way. It is the legacy of the believers who have gone before us that challenges us to venture out and walk The Way of heroic virtue.

CHAPTER TWO

TRUE NORTH

My friend Dennis Reilly acquired a really cool classic car in mint condition, and he intends to keep it that way. Just like any true car guy, he pored over the owner's manual until he knew everything about how to keep that car looking and running great. If he fails to change the oil at the recommended interval or uses the wrong kind of oil filter, he may soon have a beautiful, shiny, lawn ornament. It won't go anywhere.

For people who love cars, there is no question about utilizing the owner's manual. It's common sense, and it pays off by preserving the integrity of a beloved automobile. Yet how many of us neglect or even reject reading the owner's manual for life, the Word of God? If we don't develop an understanding of how to nourish and care for our bodies, minds, and hearts by reading the Bible and how the Church understands and applies it, our lives become as ineffective as a classic car with a burned out engine. If you hold the Bible in one hand and the *Catechism of the Catholic Church (CCC)* in the other, you will develop a pretty good understanding of how to optimize the life that God has given you.

Gregory of Nyssa said it succinctly, "The goal of the virtuous person is to become like God" (CCC 1803).[1] One of the first steps to optimizing the life God has given you is in the knowledge and practice of virtue. The *Catechism* says, "A virtue is a habitual and firm disposition to do the good. It allows the person not only to perform good acts, but to give the best of himself. The virtuous person tends toward the good with all his sensory and spiritual powers; he pursues the good and chooses it with concrete actions" (1803).

Virtue is a habit of choice. It is a practiced act of our will, and is especially powerful when we cooperate with the infusion of God's grace. It is a chosen, developed and habitual response to life situations. Notice that last line: the virtuous person chooses good "with concrete actions." In other words, the virtues are not just something to think about, they give us something to do. A surfer becomes a better surfer as he spends more time in the water and learns from his friends and experiences how to improve. It is so with the virtues too. They're actionable—which means our ability to pursue the good improves with practice!

Virtue starts with our taking all thoughts into captivity. An attitude of virtue is cultivated by our habits of thought. The discussion of the seven virtues starts with the battleground of our minds. The Bible challenges us to pursue virtue at the level of our thought life when it states, "whatever is true, whatever is honorable, whatever is just, whatever is pure, whatever is pleasing, whatever is commendable, if there is any excellence and if there is anything worthy of praise, think about these things" (Philippians 4:8).

The early Church Fathers referred to the first four virtues of justice, temperance, prudence, and fortitude as the four cardinal virtues, from the Latin root word *cardes,* which means "hinge," as in the hinge on a gate. The narrow gate to the morally good life hinges on these four virtues. The *Catechism* says:

> *Human virtues* are firm attitudes, stable dispositions, habitual perfections of intellect and will that govern our actions, order our passions, and guide our conduct according to reason and faith. They make possible ease, self-mastery, and joy in leading a morally good life. The virtuous man is he who freely practices the good. (CCC 1804)

Both believers and non-believers can aspire and grow in the four cardinal virtues. But when these natural virtues are cultivated in an environment empowered by God's grace along with the three spiritual virtues, they become supernatural. With the aid of God's supernatural grace, we are called to be superheroes—that is, we are called to be saints. As the *Catechism* says, "Human virtues acquired by education, by deliberate acts and by a perseverance ever renewed in repeated efforts are purified and elevated by divine grace. With God's help, they forge character and give facility in the practice of the good. The virtuous man is happy to practice them" (CCC 1810).

Years ago, I had a group of teenagers from a confirmation group in my home and I decided to take a poll. I asked, "How should we decide which way is true north?" The only solution they could think of without the use of a compass was to all point at the same time and then take an average of the way everyone was pointing. Their hope was that the average would be relatively close to true north.

It was amazing how some actually pointed in the opposite direction from others. There were some clusters where people pointed in the same general direction, but that resulted more from peer pressure than instinct, I suspect. They did their best to average the directions and came to a consensus. I took out my compass and revealed that they were off by twenty degrees. They all seemed pretty happy with that, but I challenged their happiness.

"How many of you have been to sea at night?" I asked.

In Hawaii, if you try to navigate from island to island and you are even a few degrees off, your next stop is at least twenty-five hundred miles away. I could see on their faces that my point had hit home: sometimes, precision is a matter of life and death. Relativity will get you nowhere on the open ocean.

And yet, relativity is heralded by our culture as the greatest of virtues, especially in matters of morality and truth. Our culture is losing its sense of true north. We are adrift with no moral compass. Our culture's only moral absolute seems to be that there is no moral absolute. (This of course is a self-contradictory statement, for they are making an absolute statement in saying there is no absolute.) The pervading idea that we can reach our destination by all pointing and then just take the average and make it our consensus, or worse yet have everyone decide for themselves, is crazy.

Once a friend of mine was serving as celestial navigator on a sailing yacht near Turkey. The captain told my friend his coordinates, which were based on his GPS, but my friend kept insisting that, according to his sextant readings, the GPS was wrong. Eventually, the captain came down to look at the navigation charts and realized that my friend had shot the stars correctly with his sextant. If they stayed true to the flawed GPS, they would have soon collided with a peninsula.

Instead of setting our course according to true north, our culture twists and turns in murky moral waters, creating our own maps to rationalize our behavior. As St. Paul said, some are "tossed to and fro and blown about by every wind of doctrine, by people's trickery, by their craftiness in deceitful scheming" (Ephesians 4:14). Even well-intentioned people navigate a course that radically misses the mark and, worse yet, others purposefully pursue their own selfish desires. In either case, that course leads into the shallow reef of destruction rather than the depth of God's wisdom and love.

The cultural compass is broken and we're adrift, far from home. With no well-formed or informed guidance system of right and wrong, our ship heads for the rocky shoals of self-deceit, ultimately ending in our own self-defeat. But we are not doomed to this tragic course. God has given us the gyroscopic guidance system of our conscience, and made understanding available to us through the Bible and the *Catechism*. It is our choice whether or not we use these gifts God has given us and allow him to steer our ship along the course of his love.

Where we spend eternity is 100 percent under our control. His Word makes our options very clear: we can cooperate with the grace that Christ merited for us on the cross, or we can reject it and keep to our own course. The way to heaven is narrow, but it is no secret. He showed us the way, as spectacularly and as clearly as he possibly could, at the cross.

The pursuit of the seven virtues is its own reward. Moses, the great legislator of the Hebrew Law, proclaimed, "You must follow exactly the path that the LORD your God has commanded you, so that you may live, and that it may go well with you" (Deuteronomy 5:33). There can be no greater pursuit of discovery and adventure than the quest for virtue that will someday bring us to our ultimate desire and absolute bliss. God challenges us to rise up, be valiant and by his power to pursue the deep adventure that is the way of heroic virtue.

CHAPTER THREE
HEAVY WATER

The twenty-plus-foot waves of Waimea Bay were monstrous enough to pound fear into the rhythm of any heart. I stood on the shoreline in a surreal state of mind, detached from reality. The giant waves dwarfed the size of the bay. The summer sounds of children frolicking in the bay's deep, calm waters were replaced by the warnings of lifeguards, called out on their bullhorns. Monolithic sets built up on the horizon. Before long, most beach-goers had abandoned the water, leaving only the most determined and daring to brave the heavy waters.

From time to time, a rescue helicopter would circle over the surfers in the lineup or zip by on its way to pull someone out of the water at another beach. I have seen these waves break bodies and take lives. Once after a horrific wipe out, my friend Scotty Perez was pulled out of the bay by a rescue copter. His arm, broken at the bicep, was held together by just a few tendons.

 I stood high on the steep shoreline, feeling the surge of water rushing past my legs and ripping back to sea, trying to suck me out with it. With each wave, my feet sank a little deeper in the sand and resolve settled a little deeper in my soul.

Waimea only breaks when the surf is huge. When all the other surf spots along the North Shore's Miracle Mile are closed out by massive, unrideable walls of water, the deeper reef of Waimea just begins to break, each wave as tantalizingly beautiful as it is deadly. Surfers will stand on the water's edge for a half hour or more in order to scope things out, our eyes locked on the ocean, our bodies, carved by hours in the ocean, coiled with energy. These moments may look meditative, but don't be deceived. We are actively engaged with what we see. Soldiers preparing for battle. Athletes focused on our strategy. As we watch the waves, we are doing recon: gauging how big the biggest wave is, timing the wave intervals, counting how many waves in a set. We are looking for the direction the swell is coming from, seeing if there is more than one swell, watching how it is breaking and on what area of the reef it is hitting. For years, we've prepared our bodies for this moment. Now, we're preparing our minds, fortifying our instincts with invaluable information.

But we can only watch for so long before mental preparation morphs into something much more sinister: fearful avoidance. The longer I stood there stewing in the juices of my own adrenaline, the shakier my body became. The shakier my body, the shakier my courage. A primal fear—a natural but deeply cautious sense of self-preservation—can sneak in. If I give it space in my head or heart, it becomes debilitating.

A lot of surfers stand on the beach like this, surfboard in hand, and never paddle out. For some reason, I always do. I held my eleven-foot-six-inch Becker big wave elephant gun surfboard under my arm and gathered up my courage along with my leg leash. At the very moment fear threatened to overwhelm me, I sprinted toward the water and leapt as high as I could to get over the shore break, landing on my surfboard and paddling with all my might.

I was met by steamroller surges of water that tried to push me back toward shore, but after a minute or so, I powered through those first few hundred yards and into the relentless force of a riptide that sent me surging out to sea. The riptide can be a big wave rider's best friend. It is like a ski lift in Aspen, propelling the rider almost effortlessly toward the top of the slope. It helped me easily paddle the rest of the way in the deep water of the channel next to *hehe nalu,* the mountaintop waves.

Instead of paddling right into the lineup, I sat in the deeper channel next to the pit where the waves were breaking. I watched one more set cycle through. There is one particular boil mark that is caused by the wave breaking over an area of the reef that is shallower then the rest. I always navigate by that boil mark. I watched the swell and saw how it was breaking on that spot to determine where I wanted my takeoff to be. I paddled into the lineup and looked out to sea, searching for the death-bomb waves. My hope was that I'd be able to successfully ride those waves, but if not, I prayed I would at least survive them. Finally, a wave approached, and I turned to paddle for it.

You cannot catch a big wave unless you paddle into it with all of your heart, strength, and mind. You have to really want to ride that wave, you have to go for it with everything you've got, and you have to have your wits about you. You need to reason through your decision of where to paddle from and when to go and when not to. You must be willing to give it everything you've got, and you have to want it.

Living a virtuous and spiritually rich life is like riding a big wave. You cannot move in the fullness of the virtues unless you reach out for God's power. You have to dedicate your heart, strength, and mind to the task at hand. The ocean is a dangerous place for those who don't respect its power or acknowledge its might. The same is true with God—his love is wild and untamable, and he isn't interested in the lukewarm who paddle out halfheartedly, distracted by the pleasures of the shore behind them. In fact, the Bible tells us that the Lord will spit out the lukewarm (Revelation 3:16). But when you fully commit, he will propel you into experiences you never dreamed of.

Do not linger on the shore. God's adventure is waiting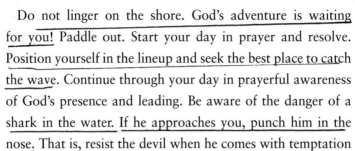
for you! Paddle out. Start your day in prayer and resolve.
Position yourself in the lineup and seek the best place to catch
the wave. Continue through your day in prayerful awareness
of God's presence and leading. Be aware of the danger of a
shark in the water. If he approaches you, punch him in the
nose. That is, resist the devil when he comes with temptation
and he will flee (see James 4:7).

Be aware of other surfers in the water. Inexperienced or reck-
less surfers can be your greatest danger. Choose wisely with
whom you spend your time during the day. Just like surfers
review their camera footage to see how they can improve,
examine your thoughts, words, and deeds to determine how
you can do better. Where you failed, seek reconciliation with
God and others.

My "car guy" friend, Dennis Reilly, has made more than
seven hundred carrier landings, a lot of them at night. He
understands the difference between the small, single-propeller
plane that I fly and the powerful jets he flies. He once told me
that what makes a jet engine so powerful is that it recycles
and speeds up the air within it. Each time it cycles, it produces
more power and speed. Power builds upon power.

This is how virtue grows, too. Each virtuous thought and
action builds upon others so that the virtue within us grows
more and more powerful. To the Greek philosophers, the word
"good" implies that something fulfills its intended purpose. A
lime tree, for example, is good if it grows perfect limes for a
gin and tonic or for key lime pie. A good Harley is one that
powers us along beautiful, winding mountain roads. If something is living up to its potential and purpose, it is good.

When God created light, he said it was good because the sun
and stars filled the universe with light, as they were intended
to do. When God created Adam and Eve, he said it was *very*

good, and they tended the garden and walked in humble relationship with God, fulfilling their purpose. The virtues, then, are good when we live in them and allow their work to be seen in us. Peter Kreeft writes,

> In its classical signification, virtue means the power of anything to accomplish its specific function; a property capable of producing certain effects: strength, force, potency.... It implies a mysterious energetic power, as in the gospel according to Mark: "Jesus immediately, knowing that virtue had gone out from him, turned and said, 'who touched my clothes?' and then said to the woman, 'your faith has cured you.'"[2]

It is in the virtue of Christ's divine nature to bring wholeness and healing, and so when the woman reached out in faith, his virtue flowed forth and fulfilled his nature.

The virtuous life builds us up more and more in the ability and agility to live in virtue. It builds up in us, by the power of the Holy Spirit, the potency to both want and to do God's will. As we rely on the power of the Holy Spirit to grow in virtue, we become more and more potent with his power, and more responsive to what life asks of us.

St. Paul had a favorite word. Was it *love*? Was it *God*? No. It was the Greek word *dynamos*, as in dynamite. He used this word, usually translated as "power," more than any other word in his writings. I ride a Harley Heritage now, but my last Harley was called a Dyna-glide. The prefix *dyna* indicates how powerful its engine was. Its rumble set off car alarms. Perhaps you sense the rumble of the voice of God deep within you right now, challenging you to seek the dynamite of the power of his love and grace in your life.

A big wave rider only rides the wave. Of himself, he cannot generate any power or move through the water with much speed or dynamic. The surfer has to want that wave and paddle with all his might to get into it. Then, he must abandon himself to the power of the wave. Likewise, we must paddle out and seek the *dynamos* of God. God sends the wave of his will, his grace, and his power. Our job is to become one with him and his will, like a surfer becomes one with the wave. Moving in the power of virtue comes from an ongoing prayer life and a reliance on and surrender to him.

Our creed at Deep Adventure Ministries states: "The most radical thing that you can do in life is to abandon yourself to the wild adventure of God's will." When you say yes to pursuing virtue, your life will never be the same. For, by saying yes, you have, in fact, invited the God of the universe to take over. He will hear you, and he will teach you and guide you; but more than that, he will actually help you. He will develop your spiritual strength and moral character. By choosing to leave the shore of relativism, you are paddling out into the heavy waters of virtue. Here, deep in the wave, you will meet God, and he will prepare you for the way of heroic virtue.

I have skydived. I have run with the bulls in Pamplona. I have even repelled out the window of my twenty-fifth-floor condo in Waikiki. But nothing comes close to the sense of trepidation I feel when I see the hehe nalu *waves rising out on the ocean more than five miles out to sea. I've paddled out almost to the lineup and am hanging back, watching the water. Excitement and foreboding fill me, and memories of close calls come flooding back to me, but out here in the lineup, my sense of resolve is even greater. I am one man, alone on my surfboard in the vast, deep, and powerful sea. Now, the only choice left to me is to turn myself over to the power of the wave and let instinct take over. I know that each wave in succession will be bigger than the one in front of it, and I could be in for a pounding.*

As the first wave approaches, I paddle up its almost-vertical face and fly out the back, barely keeping my balance. The next wave is bigger, and I can see a surfer racing down the line toward me. For his sake and mine, I need to get over that lip. My abs are firing so hard that I feel like I've been kicked in my solar plexus. Luckily, I make it out the back of the wave just as the second surfer barrels past.

As I paddle over the last wave, I catch a glimpse of two stand-up paddlers farther out to sea. One of them is kneeling and the other struggling to keep his balance. Somehow these beginners must have made it beyond the deeper channels between the reefs. They are an eighth of a mile farther out. I understand these waters, and I know the current and winds are working against them, even though they clearly don't recognize their predicament.

Instead of waiting for the next set of waves, I paddle hard to catch up with them. When I reach them, we are about a mile from shore.

I keep it casual, "How you guys doing?"

"Great." The man's response is clipped with annoyance.

I tell them what I know they don't want to hear: "The current is running strong today and the trade winds are blowing hard off shore. Are you thinking of turning back soon?"

He waves me off. "Naw. We got this."

"Why don't you turn toward shore and paddle to test the conditions? Just see how it goes?"

His female companion awkwardly turns her board around and starts to paddle. She immediately realizes that she isn't making progress at all. In fact, she is being pulled farther out to sea. A look of alarm twists her sunburned face.

"You're OK," I say. I maneuver my board toward her.

She reaches out for me with a panicked look as the strong current sends her drifting by. I call for her to grab on to the surf leash that is trailing behind my board and she desperately scoops it from the water. I feel the solid tug on my board as the weight of hers starts to pull me farther from the beach with the current.

I wave to her husband. "Can you get to her leash and hold on to it?"

"Why should I?" he sneers.

I ignore his attitude. "Because I am not going to come back out to get you," I answer firmly.

He reluctantly tries to head toward us, but as he paddles hard into the wind and current, it becomes clear that he cannot reach us. He is being swept out to sea—and fast.

The
Virtue
of
Justice

CHAPTER FOUR
GO DEEP

O ne day, early in the new millennium during the first big swell of the year, I looked toward the waves and saw one lone surfer who was deeper in the peak than anyone else.

When the first set came, I saw him paddling out to sea over wave after wave, each one bigger than the last. Finally, as the biggest wave of the set bore down on him, he faced the shore and paddled with all of his might to catch it. At the summit of a twenty-eight-foot wall of water, his board began to free fall, with only his fin and a little bit of the back of his board grabbing the hollow wave face.

Pushing the nose down, he stood up. As he got to his feet, he did something startling. He launched himself off his board and into the jaws of the wave in a perfect swan dive. Most surfers would consider this move a death drop, but he threw himself into it with total abandon. At the last moment, he straightened his arms out and pierced the face of the wave. I knew that, deep beneath the surface, he was going into the fetal position, his arms wrapped around his knees, drawing them close to his chest. Surfers do this so that our limbs are not dislocated from the violence of the wave as it shakes us like a toy in a dog's jaws.

I watched in stunned disbelief as the wave pummeled him. All I could see was the nose of his big wave gun standing in the water like a tombstone. The board was attached to his leg by the leash, though he was still being held down under more than twenty feet of water. It seemed like an eternity passed until this fearless surfer popped up, laughing loudly. With a look of exaltation, he grabbed his board and paddled to the deep channel before the next huge wave pounced on him.

This was one of my first sightings of a man who would soon become one of my best friends. If you have listened to my radio show or read my blog, you may have guessed who it was. This was Crazy Todd Robertson.

Every year, on the first big swell of the season, Crazy Todd still defies death like he did that day. His routine, while alarming to the rest of us, is his way of getting his biggest wipeout of the season over with as soon as possible. It's how he shows respect to the ocean, and acknowledges its incredible power. He embraces the beauty of the waves, and with this act of total abandonment and surrender, he acknowledges that he is at the mercy of something completely outside of his control. He is giving the ocean the justice that it has due from him.

The *Catechism* introduces the virtue of justice this way: "Justice is the moral virtue that consists in the constant and firm will to give our due to God and neighbor" (CCC 1807).

In other words, the virtue of justice is a little like the scales of justice. Justice brings balance between what is due and what is paid. Micah 6:8 calls us "to do justice, and to love kindness, and to walk humbly with your God." If I buy a collector's edition comic book on eBay, I pay the price that is due, and the seller sends me the comic book that is due. We are acting in justice, balancing the scales.

The virtue of justice in its classic sense has two focuses: justice toward God and justice toward others. Think of the vertical beam of the cross as being justice toward God and the horizontal beam as justice toward others. Where the beams intersect is where we are called to live, centered firmly in our will—that is, our determination—to show justice to God and our neighbor.

But there is, I believe, even more to that vital intersection. To fully live in the center of justice, the center of God's will, is to also show justice to our own selves. I believe this is what Jesus implies when he says, "Love your neighbor as yourself" (Mark 12:31). How can we treat others justly if we do not give ourselves what we ourselves are due? What we have due to ourselves is a life of virtue.

Christ came that we might "have life, and have it abundantly" (John 10:10). In other words, we owe it to ourselves to pursue Christ and the abundant life he offers. We can pursue the *summum bonum,* or highest good—that is, happiness, joy, and fulfillment in Christ. But most importantly, the eternal bliss of the presence of God.

The most essential justice that we owe ourselves is the gift of salvation. God planted within us a desire for happiness for a reason. The desire for happiness is, at its core, the desire for God. The fulfillment of true happiness can be found only in him. We were made for relationship with him. How mindblowing is that? The God of the universe created you for him. Yet how many neglect this great gift, which is an injustice against their own being?

If we do not love ourselves enough to pursue all that God has for us, how can we give justice to others? Without God, all we end up doing is bartering for the temporary and flawed affection of those around us. This is why I believe the selfward virtue of justice is pivotal to our ability to show justice to others. "My child, treat yourself well, according to your means, and present worthy offerings to the Lord" (Sirach 14:11).

If we start here, we provide ourselves with a solid foundation in the virtue of justice. But we cannot stop with this inward focus, of course. To fully live in the deep virtue of justice, we must live out the vertical and horizontal beams of the cross as well. That is, we must also show justice to God and to our neighbor.

A strong sense of justice stabilizes us and gives us balance in our dealings with God and man. When you drop in on a big wave, you transition from lying on your board to getting to your feet. Your feet may shift a bit as you find that perfect balance point and lean into the wave. Often, reaching into the face of the wave draws you closer to it and helps you to change your trajectory. Justice is exactly that. It is getting to your feet and finding that solid sense of the balance point by reaching out and touching the face of God in the give and take between ourselves and God, and ourselves and others. Finding this solid, stabilizing balance point of justice provides us with the stance and disposition we need to draw a clean line on the wave of life as we pursue the other virtues.

CHAPTER FIVE

SCUBA TANK THEOLOGY

I was on the fourth dive of my life—only my second day of scuba diving—when my instructor took me to the wall off of Hanauma Bay on the island of O'ahu. We were down 120 feet, and I was having a blast. Being able to move freely in three-dimensional space gave me a sense of flying, and the fish, sharks, *honu* (sea turtles), and dolphins accepted us as one of their own.

In my excitement, I forgot to conserve my oxygen. At that depth I needed more oxygen just to function normally, but I was foolishly trying to get in a cardio workout. My dive master came over to check my supply and signaled me to keep my eye on it. When he came back shortly after that, I could see his concern.

He signaled that we would have to switch tanks under water. He knew he would be much better at conserving oxygen than I was. He helped me take off my tank, and I held it while he took off his and strapped it on my back. In that moment, holding my tank in my hands and my last breath in my lungs, I realized that if the transition did not go smoothly, I would have no air at 120 feet below the surface. Thankfully, we made the switch and very slowly surfaced. Both of us made it back up about the time my tank emptied out.

All of us start our journey into the virtues at the bottom of the sea. We can swim around and explore things, but the only way we'll really be able to reach the fullness of virtuous living is by showing justice toward God. Giving God the justice he is due is our source of oxygen in the ocean of virtue: without it, we cannot live. If we don't get this right, we can't get any of the virtues right, which means we can't get life right.

In the Mass, when the priest says, "Let us give him thanks and praise," we respond, "It is right and just." It is *just* to give God thanks and praise. It truly is what he has due from us. In Jesus, God gave us far beyond what we had due from him. The reality is that we can never repay him. But we can thank him. We can praise him. We can show him the justice he has due by simply acknowledging his wisdom and strength in our lives and confessing that we would be lost at sea without his saving grace.

God breathed into Adam and gave him the oxygen of a rational and spiritual soul that was capable of knowing God. But, the first lesson that God taught Adam and Eve was justice toward him. Back in the good old days, God would come and hang out with Adam and Eve in the cool of day, the time we call *pau hana* (finish work) in Hawaii. God and Adam probably talked about Adam's plan for a new gazebo or maybe ran through lists of names for animals. Early on, God gave Adam and Eve clear boundaries. He wanted to define their relationship with him so that everything he had made and called good would remain so. Adam and Eve needed to know and respect that he was God and they were not.

Their continued existence in the perfect garden—and in the perfect relationship with God—depended on their constant and firm will to show God justice. He warned them that the day they ate of the fruit of the tree of the knowledge of good and evil, they would surely die. Literally, the word he used meant to "lose aspiration." In other words, they would lose breath. Like me, they would be stranded at the bottom of the ocean with no oxygen in their tanks.

But Adam and Eve did not resist the temptation. Satan fed their pride, and as their pride grew, their desire to show justice toward God diminished. They forgot that God was the supplier of their oxygen, and did not give him his due. And so death came. We see the first recorded physical death in the garden when God killed an animal to make the loin cloths to cover the shame that Adam and Eve felt in the new awareness of their nakedness. They were thrown out of the garden of perfect communion with God, and the entrance was blocked by a flaming sword.

The second person of the trinity, the divine Son of God, dove deep into the world that he had created. He dove deep to rescue us, to bring us oxygen. He does not just bring us a scuba tank, but breathes into us afresh with his own breath. He breathes his blessing over us: "Jesus said to them again, 'Peace be with you. As the Father has sent me, so I send you.' When he had said this, he breathed on them and said to them, 'Receive the Holy Spirit'" (John 20:21–22). Whether we want to believe it or not, we are 120 feet down with the clock ticking, but Jesus, our Dive Master, has offered to switch tanks with us.

Every morning I hold my breath for two minutes and twenty seconds during the sunrise and every night I hold it for the sunset. The longer you hold your breath, the more you feel the carbon dioxide building in your lungs, screaming for you to let it out. Without Christ, we are holding our breath indefinitely, keeping the poison inside. We are clinging to our own wants and desires, and our soul becomes sick. But when we finally breathe out the sick air of our own disposition and allow Christ to breath his Spirit into us, we are born anew. In Christ, we don't need a scuba tank, which will always run out of air. We won't need to cling to temporal things. For within our soul will be an everlasting supply of the very breath of God.

The best news is that with his supply of breath we can dive deeper and deeper into the wonder of his love through the pursuit of the virtues.

CHAPTER SIX

MAKING THINGS PONO

Surfing champion Mary Osborne and I were tandem surfing in the light of a golden California sunset, while famed photographer David Pu'u shot us from the beach. When the other surfers saw my beautiful, famous tandem partner and became aware of David on the beach, electricity crackled through the lineup. (David took the photo for the cover of this book.)

Though he was there to shoot us exclusively, some surfers saw this as their big chance to get their picture in a magazine, so they paddle-battled each other like sharks in a feeding frenzy. As we dropped in on a wave, another surfer dropped in on us. This wasn't just rude, it was a violation of the unspoken surfer code. He had committed the mortal sin of snaking another surfer. His selfish and dangerous move forced us to turn back over a barely submerged boulder. We barely missed a car-sized rock jutting out of the water.

David's camera ignored him. We paddled back out to the lineup, waiting our turn again, giving everyone else their due and their share of the waves. Finally a big wave, beautifully backlit by the setting sun, rolled toward us and we paddled into a beautiful take off. It was the shot David had been waiting for. As we began our bottom turn in front of the submerged rock, the same surfer dropped in on us again.

This time, there was no avoiding him. I had already buried my rail deep into the turn. My board shot between his legs, scooping him up and depositing him on the nose of my board. He flailed like a dying cockroach as he lay on his back, looking up at Mary's shocked smile, until he slid off to the side of our board and into the water. We rode past him and executed a beautiful lift with Mary arching upside-down over my head.

As we paddled in, David's hysterical laughter greeted us. "Don't worry you guys. Justice will be served. He wanted to be famous and I am going to make him famous," he said, his eyes glinting with his usual mischief.

Soon, the picture of that snake flailing on his back appeared in a major surf magazine and his friends never let him live it down. He'd gotten his moment of fame, but the consequences of his lack of consideration were on display instead of his surfing skill. He had sought his own glory and had no care or sense of justice toward us.

The other surfers gave us the dignity and respect that was our due. The other surfers acted in the virtue of justice. Justice toward others is giving another what they have due from us. Preserving their dignity, respecting their personal boundaries, never making someone feel small or as if they are beneath you is giving them their due. Balancing the scales in transactions between each other is giving them their due. For example, employees owe their employers a fair day's work, just as employers owe them a fair day's pay. Justice toward others is mutual consideration, respect, and goodwill. In Hawaii, we call it making things *pono*.

The *Catechism* clearly defines justice toward others: "Justice towards men disposes one to respect the rights of each and to establish in human relationships the harmony that promotes equity with regard to individual persons and to the common good. The just man...is distinguished by habitual right thinking and uprightness in conduct toward his neighbor" (CCC 1807).

This is the essence of Jesus's teaching when he says, "In everything do to others as you would have them do to you; for this is the law and the prophets" (Matthew 7:12). But as Christians, the scales of justice place a bigger burden on us, for we have been forgiven and have a relationship with the loving God of the universe. Do you remember these words of Scripture? "Everyone to whom much has been given, much will be required" (Luke 12:48). In Christ, we have been given eternal life. What is greater than this? Is it really unreasonable to think that God might expect us to demonstrate this gift and to show his great love in our daily lives beyond what we would normally think of as balancing the scales of justice?

It is not enough to say, "I fulfilled my commitment to my fellow man. To the extent possible, I am self-reliant, not a burden to anyone; and I don't steal free Internet or download pirated movies. I'm a good person. In regards to others, I do nothing wrong."

Really? Does following basic rules, generally being a good person, and doing the bare minimum in regards to charity and compassion really seem like a fitting display of gratitude for the gift of eternal life? Cut off the last word from the sentence above and read it again. It would read, "In regard to others, I do *nothing*—" God has a calling in service to others for you that fits you perfectly and that only you can fulfill.

One of our staff members picked up a copy of my book *Deep in the Wave: A Surfing Guide to the Soul* at a bookstore somewhere in Wisconsin on his way to compete in a stand-up paddle race. Now he has become an integral part of our Deep Adventure Ministries. Before joining us, he worked for a supermarket produce section, and each night was in charge of throwing out the rejected produce. Reasons for rejecting produce vary from rot to only having a small bruise. He found that a lot of produce was rejected for very small blemishes that didn't impact the nutritional value of the item.

He did nothing wrong by doing his job. But it began to bother him that he was regularly throwing away perfectly good food. He was showing his employer justice in that he continued to do his work, but he had a sense that he was being called to an even deeper display of virtue. He started seeing a van for a homeless shelter in the neighborhood drive by, and because Justin was already open to and seeking deep virtue, the Holy Spirit prompted him one day to chase the van down. He arranged a daily rendezvous to provide the shelter with the edible but rejected food.

What many may see as an act of charity is in actuality an act of justice. Our fallen world's economic distribution system is so far from just that what we call an act of charity—providing food for the homeless, for example—is really a demonstration of those who have been given much showing justice to those in need. We have a responsibility to balance the scales, to show love where there is hate, to provide food where there is hunger, and to protect what is vulnerable. If life has treated you well, then justice demands that you help balance the scales.

Mother Teresa suggested that we pray each day to see Jesus in the people around us, especially those in need. To see Christ in others is to see their humanity and their deep value to God. Someone once told Pope Francis that his words had inspired him to give a lot more to the poor. Pope Francis's response was to challenge the man not to just give money, but to roll up his sleeves, get his hands dirty, and actually reach out and help.

Pope Francis and Mother Teresa were both upholding the words of Christ when he said, "Truly, I tell you, just as you did it to one of the least of these who are members of my family, you did it to me" (Matthew 25:40). Do you see? When we reach out to those in need, we are truly reaching out to Jesus. We owe an infinite and eternal debt to Jesus for he gives his infinite self to us and makes us partakers in his divine nature and eternal life. When we do good to others, we are not doing more than our fair share. We are acting in justice.

What we do to the least, we are doing to Jesus, and to him we owe the donation of our total self.

One of the most profoundly effective ways you can enact justice is by giving yourself to intercessory prayer for the needs that you see as you go through your day. Just like Adam, we all have a *kuleana* (responsibility) in the garden around us to which we must attend. Adam was charged with caring for the garden and making springs flow. The garden was his turf, so to speak. It was his to care for. In the same way, our garden is ours to care for as we wish.

That is why God often waits for us to pray in intercession and supplication before he acts. He has given us dominion, and he respects our dignity. He waits for us to ask for his help and guidance. The Bible promises that "the prayer of the righteous is powerful and effective" (James 5:16). And so as you walk through your day, try to really see others as God sees them and pray for their needs. Pray for springs of the Holy Spirit to flow forth in their lives.

It is interesting to me how the more I pray the prayer, "Lord, not my will but yours be done," the more aware and empathetic I am of the needs of those around me. I have learned that it is not necessarily God's will that I get the perfect parking spot, nor is it just for me to hurry my step so I can get in line before someone else. I have had to learn to recognize the Jesus in others and show them justice by acknowledging that they may need things to be a little easier that day.

Justice means to be less concerned about the outcome of things than about the means to accomplish them. Justice calls us to live with our eyes, ears, and hearts open, intentionally seeking ways we can show God's love through acts of compassion and charity. To be deep in the virtue of justice is to be deeply in tune with God's incredible love for his creation. If we want to walk in the way of heroic virtue, then understanding justice—and showing it toward God, toward others, and toward ourselves—is a vital first step. With our souls planted firmly on the bedrock of justice, we can pursue the other virtues.

CHAPTER SEVEN

THE WAY OF HEROIC VIRTUE: FRIAR ANTONIO DE MONTESINOS

riar Antonio's voice boomed out an opening salvo
that was as shocking and terrifying to the Spanish
authorities present as the cannons exploding from the
sixteenth-century warships were to the native population of
Hispaniola. He stood with his hand raised close to his mouth
like a megaphone, making his shouts louder—a pose that
has been immortalized in a statue that stands on the seafront
of the Santa Domingo harbor. Friar Antonio's words were
unflinching:

> In order to make your sins known to you…I who am a voice
> of Christ crying in the wilderness…for this is going to be
> the strangest voice that you have ever heard, the harshest
> and hardest and most awful and most dangerous,…this
> voice says that you are in mortal sin…for the cruelty and
> tyranny you use in dealing with these innocent people….
> For with excessive work you demand of them they fall ill
> and die, or rather you kill them with your desire to extract
> gold.[3]

Can you imagine the uproar among the merchants and the
conquistadores at these words? The young friar shouted
out their sins to them in front of the very natives that they
abused. His voice was like a rogue wave ramming against one
of their warships. In front of the whole congregation, he listed
their crimes. He showed justice boldly, acknowledging the
humanity of the abused and neglected natives, and speaking
against those inflicting injustice.

They were trapped with nowhere to hide from the sword of
the Spirit that the young friar brandished against them. Those

in authority who had committed so many crimes against the people were like Belteshazzar at his feast when the hand wrote on the wall, "You have been weighed on the scales and found wanting" (Daniel 5:27).

The Spanish authorities angrily threatened the friar and demanded a retraction. The next Sunday, only nineteen years after Columbus had claimed the Americas for Spain, the young friar humbly walked up to the lectern and took a long look at his notes. He then raised his hand to his mouth and blasted out more words of warning. Because he saw no repentance in the authorities for what he called mortal sins, he told his friars not to hear their confessions.

The voice of this one friar crying out in the wilderness boomed all the way to the courts of King Ferdinand, where soon the Franciscans echoed the same explosive accusations. The king called together a group of theologians and legal minds to develop what was essentially the beginning of international law. Friar Antonio saw the persecution of the indigenous people of what is now Haiti and the Dominican Republic, and he could not remain silent. The virtue of justice that was deep within him propelled him to speak out boldly, caring little for his own well-being, in order to protect those who were vulnerable to an unjust authority.

One voice, crying out for justice, can make a difference. Friar Antonio's actions resulted not only in a balancing of the injustice being done to the indigenous peoples of those islands, but became the basis for the international law concerning human rights today. His act of standing up as a solitary voice is still heard throughout the world.

"Hang on tight!" I tell the woman in the water, and turn my board toward her husband. I have to paddle hard downwind and down current to catch up with him. Once I reach him, I paddle past his board and then across the front so he can reach for her trailing leash.

I instruct them to lay their paddles on their boards and keep their bodies prone to cut their wind resistance. I turn toward the shore, my eyes locking on my target and resolve setting in like it has done so many times before in similar situations. I remember paddling the treacherous thirty-mile channel between the islands of Molokai and O'ahu. Then, it was a matter of one paddle stroke after another, and timing the sets. The same is true now.

We are far out, and everything is working against us. But the only thing about this that is truly unpredictable is the two of them. Will they listen, follow instructions, and keep their cool? Rescuing just one person is easy. But saving two people, especially one who is obstinate and potentially uncooperative, might put them both in peril.

I can see the swell continuing to build. Each set of waves that rolls under us is bigger than the last, and yet we are paddling toward the ferocious impact zone where things are going to get a lot worse before they get better. There is something both majestic and terrifying about seeing the back of a fifteen-foot wave, and something humbling about the sound of it exploding on the reef. As it lifts you, it is like being in God's hands. The awe-inspiring feeling of such incredible power moving beneath impresses on you how small you really are.

I kneel down and begin paddling for the gap in the reef. There is only one gap in that area—between Paradise and Threes—that can offer us hope of a safe passage toward shore. I must navigate carefully, timing our run through it perfectly. Would they have the stamina to paddle fast and hard the moment I tell them to?

"Try not to paddle until I tell you to," I say. "I need you to conserve your energy for when we make it to the reef."

The natural cut in the reef is caused by an underwater fresh spring. The sailing catamarans used the cut in the reef to get out between the waves, but the last of them headed toward the safety of their harbor long before the swell got this big. I can see the channel water is not quite deep enough to allow the waves to slip through without breaking.

We are going to have to time it perfectly to get through, or I will have to paddle another half mile back toward Diamond Head before the next gap in the reef will allow us in. Meanwhile, the swell will be building even bigger.

Still, I don't have much choice. I have to try this gap and hope that the waves cooperate. With the dead weight of two passengers—now both obviously frightened—dragging behind me, I bend forward and sink my paddle deep into the ocean. I pull hard, using the strength of my whole body as I propel us toward our destination. I can't help but smile, thinking that my guardian angel and I have been through this before.

"I guess I like to make things interesting for you," I say, my words disappearing into the wind and waves.

As if in response, the ocean roars as another wave explodes on the reef in front of us. The safety of shore suddenly seems farther away.

The
Virtue
of
Prudence

CHAPTER EIGHT

GO FOR IT

Over the years, I've been privileged to surf with some of the best and toughest people in the surfing and water rescue world. One of these men, Archie Kalepa, has also become one of my good friends. Archie is a legendary waterman and is head of ocean safety on Maui. He has pioneered some of the most daring water rescue tactics used today, in which a Jet Ski is used for rescues when the waves are dangerously big and fast. Archie is also one of the most accomplished big wave riders and tandem surfers in the world.

His expertise and dedication to safety indicates how aware he is that he, too, is subject to the ocean's deadly power. A few years ago, Archie had the worst wipeout of his life. Suddenly a forty-foot wave pitched and Archie was driven into the pit where a wall of water crushed him and held him down under a relentless series of waves for nearly five minutes. His partner carefully worked his Jet Ski toward where he thought the surf would be pushing Archie. It's a tough, even helpless feeling for the Jet Ski partner waiting for his buddy to surface. He has the urge to rev his engine and fly everywhere, looking for the surfer; but a prudent Jet Skier knows not to do this. Surfers have been nearly killed when they suddenly surfaced right in the path of their frantic partner.

As the minutes passed, his partner broke into tears, his eyes locked on the surface of the waves. Below the water, Archie relaxed his body as much as he could in order to conserve his oxygen. He knew there was no sense trying to fight the power of the waves that kept driving him down. He needed to go in the fetal position and just wait out the onslaught, hoping his air would not completely run out.

But this set of waves was brutal. Archie began to think that, this time, he wasn't going to make it. He thought of his wife and his beautiful child. A feeling of peace came over him as he surrendered himself to death, but suddenly he felt the relentless downward pressure let go and he began to swim with all his might toward the bright sunlight above. He kicked for the surface—forty feet, then thirty, then twenty. His lungs ached, screaming for him to release the poisonous carbon dioxide trapped within them. Finally, he broke through the surface and screamed as he let out the sick air in his chest and inhaled fresh oxygen.

Archie scanned the horizon to see if another set of waves was about to dump on him, but instead he saw his tow-in partner coming at full throttle to rescue him. His partner's sobs turned to tears of joy as he reached down and grabbed Archie, pulling him onto the Jet Ski with him.

Though big wave riders challenge huge surf, they approach it with tremendous prudence. Archie and his partner have trained endlessly together in heavy conditions. They know when to drop into a big wave and when not to, and they have developed countless rescue strategies.

They check and recheck their surf gear and their Jet Ski. They review the buoy and weather reports to determine swell direction and trends, and they study the reefs to see if there is more than one swell running. They know the dangers and are actively and intimately aware of the ever-changing conditions.

To outsiders, big wave riders seem like lunatics. They willingly put themselves right in the middle of the most dangerous ocean conditions. Many people think big wave riders have a death wish, but the opposite is true. Their go-for-it attitude is really a *life* wish. They want to live to the fullest. They want to squeeze every ounce of life out of each moment. To do that, they have to have their wits about them, and they have to constantly develop their physical, mental, and emotional strength. In other words, they must be prudent.

The *Catechism* says, "Prudence is the virtue that disposes practical reason to discern our true good in every circumstance and to choose the right means of achieving it" (1806). St. Thomas Aquinas took his cue from Aristotle when he wrote that prudence is "right reason in action."[4] Prudence is what guides our actions in wisdom and righteousness (see Proverbs 8:12).

Prudence is not weakness or timidity: As the *Catechism* tells us, "It is called *auriga virtutum* (the charioteer of the virtues); it guides other virtues by setting rule and measure" (CCC 1806). Prudence isn't shaped by fear, but by courage. In fact, you don't even need prudence unless you are going to be bold.

Abandoning yourself to God's will requires a prudent boldness. It means you go against the norm. If you are going to stay inside your comfort zone, you don't need prudence at all—you just need a footrest. God is like a wild man. Take a look at nature or even into space at black holes and supernovas. There's nothing quiet or timid about God's creation. And there's nothing quiet or timid about his will.

Prudence is like a big wave rider's Jet Ski partner. It takes you out to the big waves, supports you, and brings you safely back to shore. Look at what the *Catechism* says again: "[Prudence] guides other virtues by setting rule and measure." Understanding the conditions, knowing the dangers, and familiarizing yourself with the current of life is crucial to your journey into the virtues. Without prudence, we cannot fully experience God's plan for us. Without prudence, we are lost beneath the crushing waves, or worse, left sunning ourselves on the shores of mediocrity.

We need to let prudence be the charioteer holding the reigns to the power of our passions, directing us through life's potential pitfalls. Charioteers have to be strong, courageous, and in balance. They are not timid. They lead the charge into battle. Likewise, prudence can be our most powerful ally in battle. The charioteer of prudence stands up above the fray of the infantry and sees how the battle is going. Let the bold wisdom of prudence guide your chariot.

CHAPTER NINE
COLLAPSED PARACHUTE

Skydiving is actually one of the easiest things in the world to do. We learn the basic skills of skydiving as toddlers when we fall down. You do not even need to know the "gravity" of the situation. It takes no knowledge or skill or prudence to skydive—unless, of course, you want to do it more than once. Prudent skydivers—that is, those who want to live—go through training, extensive preparation, and an entire pre-jump checklist before they even get on the plane.

My ninja sensei, Bill Poett, and a couple of other guys from our dojo were all preparing for our first jump. We were not doing the typical first jump where you tandem jump, meaning you are attached to an instructor who, in turn, is strapped to the parachute. We would not be attached to anyone when we jumped. We were doing something they called an accelerated free fall, an ominous combination of words. Bill was one guy you would not want to have to fight, but in a fight between him and the ground, the ground would win.

We started our class early in the morning, but we did not make our first jump until the sun was setting. We all laughed and joked throughout the morning classes so much that the instructor told us he felt compelled to use the word "death" more than he had for any other class. Around noon, we walked out of the jump school for a break and looked up to see a streamer fluttering through the sky. We pointed up.

"Guys, isn't that a parachute with no one attached?" I asked.

We soon learned that a jumper's chute had not deployed properly and she had to cut it away and use her reserve chute. The sight of that flimsy fabric falling to the earth like a giant autumn leaf put the reality of skydiving into perspective for us.

For the rest of the day, our attitude in the jump school became deadly serious. We were all nervous. One person in our group—whom I will not mention by name because I told Bill that I would not reveal this about him—had to go to the bathroom about every thirty minutes. He was like a little kid who gets overexcited at Disneyland. Except this Disneyland could get him killed, and he knew it. (To his credit, Bill has made more than a hundred jumps since then.)

That lone, falling parachute drove a very simple lesson home for all of us that day: if you want to skydive, everyone involved in the jump has to be prudent. You must be in good health, of sound mind, and of clear judgment in order to jump. Even having one drink before a jump could put you at risk. Just as the plane's pilot goes through a full preflight check list, so does the jumper. Everything is checked by you and then double checked by a partner. Once the checklist is verified twice, the thumbs-up signal is given by each partner. Only then are you good to go.

I have never forgotten the lesson that parachute taught me. We are meant to live boldly, to take risks, and dive deeply into the adventure of God's will. But we can't do so foolishly. We must develop prudence along with our courage. We must strive for wisdom, seek discernment, and quest for knowledge through dedication to God's Word, prayer, and sacrament. St. Bernard of Clairvaux said that "prudence is the mother of strength," meaning prudence produces the strength we need to live boldly.[5] God also promises us protection through prudence: Prudence will watch over you; and understanding will guard you" (Proverbs 2:11).

The *Catechism* expands on this idea: "It is prudence that immediately guides the judgment of conscience. The prudent man determines and directs his conduct in accordance with his judgment. With the help of this virtue we apply moral principles to particular cases without error and overcome doubts about the good to achieve and the evil to avoid" (1806). In other words, prudence seeks out the truly good in all decisions, especially in moral decisions. Through this virtue, we are guided to make *Christ-like* decisions as opposed to *convenient* decisions. Instead of being ruled by our whims, we are guided by our conscience. Pope Emeritus Benedict XVI said, "Prudence will make you patient with yourself and with others, courageous and firm in decisions, merciful and just, concerned solely with your salvation and the salvations of your brothers."[6]

I admit that, for me, prudence is a bit like Scotch. It is an acquired taste. I learned prudence the hard way, as I tend to move on impulse and often mistake my own presumption for God calling me to step out in faith.

The morning of our first jump, my buddies and I were distracted and foolish. Thankfully, our jump instructor had enough prudence to patiently continue to drive the importance of his lesson home. Instead of kicking us out, he kept passing his wisdom on until we were finally able to hear it. He got our attention by saying to us—more forcefully than he had ever said to any other group—"If you do this wrong, you are going to die." That's a wake-up call to anyone with impulse challenges. It forces you to consider the actual ramifications and then refocus your desire from the temporary satisfaction to the true good. Our jump master was concerned with our safety and made sure we were prepared. Because of him, all of us—including Bill—were able to make and survive our jump that day.

Prudence is not clever. It is not manipulative. Do not mistake it for being calculating or conniving. Prudence, on the contrary, usually brings simple clarity. To move in prudence is not always easy. Prudence humbly and reverentially puts God first. Every breath breathes in "not my will" and breathes out "but thy will be done, Lord." Jesus was constantly turning conventional wisdom on its head and pressing for a new paradigm, and he did so almost easily, by way of prudence.

The ultimate goal of the charioteer of prudence is for us to make decisions that order our lives so that we may gain eternal life and lead others to do the same. If you have a desire to pursue God's perfect will, then you will be required to be bold. Remember, God is not timid and neither are his people. In fact, they are the gnarliest, most daring people you will ever meet. Look at Peter, stepping out of the boat, or David, running full speed at Goliath with only a slingshot. Seeking first the kingdom of God will often put us in a path riddled with great obstacles and conflict. But the Word of God says, "I will go before you and level the mountains" (Isaiah 45:2). It's exciting to boldly follow him and see mountains leveled. But we must seek wisdom along the way so that we may be prudent with each step and accomplish our mission.

CHAPTER TEN
THE WAY OF HEROIC VIRTUE: KIMO MIRANDA

Kimo knew something had gone seriously wrong. They had been working as a team of three, harvesting coral while scuba diving at depths of more than 130 feet. As he dove, Kimo saw one of his friends surfacing and signaling with a slashing movement across his throat. It was the sign for trouble down deep.

Kimo propelled himself downward, not knowing what he would find, but certain that one of his best friends was in serious danger. He soon found himself swimming through a blood cloud. When the visibility cleared, he saw the upper torso of a body slowly drifting toward the surface. He knew the other half of his friend was in the belly of shark. Holding his friend's remains close with one arm, Kimo was numb with shock as he made his way to the surface.

Though he had been an ocean safety lifeguard for many years, Kimo was now determined to redouble his efforts to develop his ocean safety skills. He could not bring his friend back to life, but maybe he could save others.

Response time is critically important in ocean rescues. Getting from point A to point B is often the difference between life and death. Minutes aren't the issue. *Seconds* are. Kimo wanted to develop better techniques and new tools that would shave off precious seconds in response times, saving lives.

Kimo understood better than most that prudence is key to a successful rescue. There is a Hawaiian adage that says it is usually the person who rashly jumps in to save their friend that becomes the drowning victim. It became Kimo's mission to educate ocean rescuers in prudence, teaching them wisdom and discernment so that they could avoid rash reactions to emergencies.

Thanks to his determination, Kimo and his friends became the first to employ Jet Skis with sleds attached so that rescuers could reach a victim quickly and then hoist them onto the sled so that CPR could be performed right there in the ocean. Kimo also spent a lot of time with the older watermen, learning from their experiences. He increased his physical training, too, swimming three miles in rough water nearly every day. He quit smoking, limited his drinking, and adopted a healthy diet.

He arose early one morning in 2002 to begin his usual training regimen. Before he could start, his phone rang. A fisherman had been dragged out to sea by a huge wave from a rock cliff. Kimo, whose crew had come to be known as the *Nalu Guardians* or the "Guardians of the Sea," was the fisherman's only hope.

Kimo instructed the caller as he rushed from his room, "Tell the family that no one is to jump in and swim to the rescue. That will just make my job harder. I don't want to have to do two rescues."

He drove his four-wheel Kawasaki Mule down to the garage and attached the Jet Ski trailer before heading straight to the beach. There was no time to go to his normal launching site. He would have to power from the beach right through the heavy surf. He gave one of the men on the beach a two-way radio.

"Keep running along the cliff. Try to keep up with him as he is being swept. Keep him in sight so you can radio me where he is," he instructed.

As Kimo drove down to the beach, he wisely called for backup. He knew the fisherman was being swept down the coast by strong currents in an area that is the home of the *manu*, the tiger shark. The memory of his friend's death ripped through his soul, but Kimo was determined.

The area where the man had been seen was on a reef line where the water depth varied from five feet to a few inches. Kimo would have to work his way along this same treacherous reef, but he had been preparing for this day. He knew every coral head and every deeper channel. He had scouted all of the locations that were part of his *kuleana (responsibility)*, practicing for emergencies he hoped would never come. Emergencies just like this.

The radio crackled, "He has been thrown up on the *a'a*!"

The word *a'a* comes from the sound a person makes when stepping on the brittle, razor-sharp edges of a certain type of lava field. Kimo knew the fisherman was being ripped to shreds.

As Kimo came around the corner, he saw the man being whipped around on a rocky ledge. The victim had been tossed around by the surf for nearly a half hour. Kimo could see deep gashes and lacerations from the sharp lava all over his body. If he did not get him off that ledge soon, the man would not survive.

During the lulls between sets, he powered in close to the ledge and yelled at the man to jump into the water and swim. But the man was in shock and kept clinging to the rocks. Over the sound of the surf, Kimo heard the whine of an engine. It was his backup team. Kimo jetted out to meet the boat, and one of the rescuers jumped onto Kimo's Jet Ski. Kimo climbed in back, assuming the rescue position.

"Time the sets," Kimo yelled, "Get me within a hundred feet of the ledge if you can. When the time is right, I will swim to him and then jump off the ledge with this guy. You gotta come in and get us."

The prudence of taking his long rough-water swims had given him the strength he needed to push through the riptide and reach the victim. He held the man close, eyed the incoming waves, and then waved to his partner before jumping from the ledge. When the Jet Ski reached them, they put the man on the sled and raced back toward shore and a waiting ambulance. Along the way, Kimo worked to stabilize the victim and to stop the flow of blood from the worst of the cuts.

That day, all of Kimo's training and preparation paid off. He and his comrades were able to make wise decisions and effect a heroic rescue while minimizing their own risk. Prudence was the charioteer of that Jet Ski.

Sooner than I hope, I see an incoming swell that takes my breath away. Its lip is already feathering, even at more than a mile out to sea. The rogue wave is rising up and bearing down on us.

When the waves are this big, the huge dimensions throw off your sense of how fast they are moving. They seem sometimes to move in slow motion until they come right up on you. This set has that feeling, but my experience tells me it is moving toward us like a freight train. I make a turn back out to sea. Our only hope is to get out to deeper water before these waves can break on us.

I yelled to them, "Stay low, but I need you to paddle with one of your hands as you hang onto the leash with the other. As strong as you can!"

They can sense the urgency in my voice and respond quickly. The man has a look of consternation on his face. I know that he is wondering why I want us to paddle away from the beach. His face lights up with shock when he suddenly sees the oncoming swell. Whether fear or thrill motivates him, I don't know, but he ignores my instructions and lets go of his wife's leash in an every-man-for-himself type of move. I will do my best to help him, but I cannot allow his actions to put his wife's life in any more danger than she is already in.

He paddles with both hands as furiously as he can toward the oncoming wave, but his strokes do not go deep enough. He looks like he's doggie paddling. It won't be enough.

The wave is hollowing out in front of us, about ready to throw, as we paddle straight up its face.

"Hang on tight with both hands!" I instruct the woman.

In an instant, I fly over the lip and out the back of the wave, feeling the tug on my leash as the water tries to suck her backward over the falls. But she holds fast and we both make it *over. I look over in time to see him roll off his board as the lip passes over him. He bobs up the other side, but his board does not. The relief he feels will be short lived. I know that any moment now he will feel the pull from the leash as his board is pulled under. If he's lucky, the leash will break; if it holds, there's a good chance he will be sucked under with it.*

I continue paddling out with her, keeping an eye on him. I count the seconds to myself, watching him. Then, in a heart-beat I see him pulled under as if a shark has taken hold of him. He is going to have a bad time, but he will have to deal with it on its own. I can't help him with her in tow.

Then the strangest thing happens. The board pops out the back of the wave tail-first, and so does he.

I'm surprised and yell, "Paddle!"

He pulls himself up on the board, barely able to paddle. His arm strength is shot.

The next wave is upon us, sucking us up toward its cornice. Once again, she and I glide over it. This time, he barely makes it over too. Seven more waves bear down on us, and seven times we make it over.

When the set finally passes, I signal for the man to get back to us. I can see that he is exhausted as his arms flap like wet noodles.

"Hang on again, and both of you rest. We will need you to paddle again soon." To him I add, "Good job! But stay tight with us. We need to stay together."

He raises his head in acknowledgment and then rests it on the board, too tired to protest.

The beach is about a half a mile away. We had been making good progress, but now I will have to paddle hard to make up for the distance we just lost. The lifeguards are busy handling their own rescues. We will have to keep going alone.

I make a decision to stay with my original plan and try to make it through the first cut in the reef, but I see the waves are closing out the deep channel. I pull my paddle hard against the mounting wind and the current. I am going to have to play a game of tag with the sets of waves, avoiding the cleanup sets but using the smaller sets to give us a little push.

I start singing a silly pirate song out loud, hoping they'll think I'm not worried. After five minutes, we regain the distance we had lost. I look back over my shoulder, relieved to see there is no sign of another set.

It is now or never. I paddle hard into the no man's land of the impact zone.

PART FOUR

The
Virtue
of
Temperance

CHAPTER ELEVEN

NEW SOCKS

After a day of surfing the icy waters of Ventura County Line, my friends and I grabbed our usual tables near the back deck of Neptune's Net. My friend, Cap, lit up a cigar as if it might actually warm him up. We all liked to think of ourselves as pirates, but really we were just a bunch of scalawags.

Duck-diving under the waves as we paddled out had frozen our brains with the pain of ice cream headaches, and now we sat huddled together, chilled to the bone. We all had our sweatshirts and blue jeans on but I realized that, being the rebels we all thought we were, none of us were wearing shoes. We were renegade pirates, freezing in our flip-flops.

Because my toes were so cold, the thought of warm socks filled me with reverie. A tremendously deep insight hit me, and I decided to drop the sage pearl on my friends: "That's all a man really needs, you know."

I paused for emphasis and they turned to give me their full attention, with the very same look they would have given me if I had belched loudly.

"That's all a man really needs, you know: new, soft socks."

I wasn't just talking about socks, of course. I was introducing the idea of temperance, or self-mastery. By acknowledging that a man only needed socks, I was really thinking of the need to simplify our lives and let go of our attachment to things. As St. Paul said, "Let all men know your forbearance" (Philippians 4:5, RSV). Self-mastery means not falling into the trap of more.

At first they looked at me like I was a mad man, but their look soon turned to that of "Grasshopper" on the old *Kung Fu* television show when he listens to his ancient and wise master. Then, like so many of C.S. Lewis's obsequious Dufflepuds, they all enthusiastically agreed. Wally started it out, "Yes! Yes! Yes! That is all you really need—a new pair of socks."

The next weekend, the pirates gathered again after a surf, proudly showing off our new socks, worn with our flip-flops. We were all so pleased and contented with our newfound joy of moderation. Then someone said, "You know, besides socks, you really need a bucket. You never know when you are going to need a bucket. You need something to put your socks in."

The next weekend we all arrived at the parking lot at about the same time. As I got out of my car, a girl burst up the cliff from the beach yelling, "Please! Please! Does anyone have a bucket?"

Instantly, each of us reached into our car and grabbed our buckets, extending them to her in an eight-bucket salute. We were superheroes. We shouted in unison, "Yes! I have a bucket!"

"There are a ton of star fish all in one place. I want some for my aquarium." She walked down the line of extended buckets like a general inspecting the troops and finally selected the perfect one. We were underwhelmed by her emergency, but still felt proud of the virtue we had all shown in having a bucket at the ready.

"Yep, that's all we need: new socks and a bucket," said Cap.

Then Wally spoke up, "And a surf board. New socks, a bucket, and a surfboard."

To which someone added, "And surf wax."

"Yes! Yes!" We all agreed, smug in our new-found temperance.

"That's all you need. And a sailboat."

In the next half hour, our list of bare necessities expanded to a list of hundreds of things: a powerboat, a Harley, and on and on. Finally I summed it up, "A man's true happiness can be measured by the total number of fins and pistons he owns—twenty, of course, being the minimum number."

This principle settled everything and we all went back to discussing who got the wave of the day and how great we used to be.

Without realizing it, we had moved from temperance to temptation. From contentment to coveting. We had fallen into the trap of more. There is something in the soul of humanity that always wants something more and is never satisfied. The virtue of temperance is the self-mastery to enjoy pleasure without craving it. It is moderating our appetites so that we control them instead of them controlling us.

Our group of rebel pirates had forgotten that "there is great gain in godliness combined with contentment; for we brought nothing into the world, so that we can take nothing out of it" (1 Timothy 6:6). St. Paul continues, "But those who want to be rich fall into temptation and are trapped by many senseless and harmful desires that plunge people into ruin and destruction" (1 Timothy 6:9).

What started as a moderate desire for socks turned into a litany of "needs," none of which were truly necessary to our survival, and none that could truly fulfill us. Jesus said, "My food is to do the will of him who sent me" (John 4:34). Jesus understood that, unless a man first be filled with God, everything else he tries to fill himself with only breeds emptiness. God alone is the fulfillment of our deepest desire. This is the key to living the virtue of temperance.

The *Catechism* defines this virtue clearly:

Temperance is the moral virtue that moderates the attraction of pleasures and provides balance in the use of created goods. It ensures the will's mastery over instincts and keeps desires within the limits of what is honorable. The temperate person directs the sensitive appetites toward what is good and maintains a healthy discretion. "Do not follow your inclination and strength, walking according to the desires of your heart" (Sirach 5:2). Temperance is often praised in the Old Testament. "Do not follow your base desires, but restrain your appetites" (Sirach 18:30). In the New Testament, it is called "moderation" or "sobriety." We ought "to live sober, upright, and godly lives in this world (Titus 2:12)." (*CCC* 1809)

Original sin has inserted a great gap between what our fallen nature wants, and what we really need. When the souls of Adam and Eve rebelled against God, the bodies of Adam and Eve rebelled against their own souls and they fell into the concupiscence of inordinate and disordered desires. Like Adam and Eve, we've forgotten for whom we were really made. There is no fulfillment in the epicurean seeking of pleasure and avoidance of pain. This only breeds more emptiness.

Satan tries to keep us busy with the noise of the pleasures of life. On the contrary, the very first lesson that our contemplative saints taught us was detachment from temporal things. That is not to say material things are bad. It's not that we shouldn't enjoy the good things God has created and has provided for us in our life. But we must not cling to them.

When surfers turn their backs on the *aina* (land) and paddle out, we are turning our backs on the temporal things. Unlike the changeless ocean-scape, the land is always subject to humanity's impact of new developments and deteriorating buildings. In a sense, it represents all we cling to, all we must leave behind to venture into God's will. Likewise, a surfer never turns his back on the *makai*, the ocean. He leaves behind the things that change from day to day, the worries and cares of the world, and he paddles out to that deep and unchanging ocean.

When I say surfers leave the land behind, I mean it in several ways. Of course, we leave the physical land. But we also leave behind the things that are our "identity" to the rest of the world. We can surf with other members of the surf tribe for decades and know them well at a soul level, but never know what they did for a living because making money is not what we call living.

The ocean of God's will is where we must keep our eyes, scanning the horizon for that desired perfect wave. The only thing we can infinitely desire is an infinite being. More of God is the only desire that we can give our whole hearts to. If we desire God first and foremost, we will never fall into the trap of wanting more. John 4:14 promises, "those who drink of the water that I will give them will never be thirsty."

We live in a world full of temptation. Every day, there is something new, something enticing, something dangerous we can get our hands on. And despite our best efforts, we often find ourselves struggling as St. Paul did: "I do not understand my own actions. For I do not do what I want, but I do the very thing I hate" (Romans 7:15). We may start out on the way of self-mastery only wanting new socks, but before long, we find ourselves desiring a whole list of things. Of our own strength, we fail to live in moderation. Our disordered desires mutiny against our own will. The inmates of concupiscence have taken over the asylum.

Jesus provides the only prescription. He did not say to decrease our desire. Rather, he tells us to increase our desire, but to direct that desire toward God. He instructs us: "Love the Lord your God with all your heart, and with all your soul, and with all your strength, and with all your mind" (Luke 10:27). He goes on to promise, "Do this, and you will live" (Luke 10:28). Like David—who knew a thing or two about giving way to his wrong desires—our prayer should be: "One thing have I asked of the Lord, that will I seek after; to live in the house of the Lord all the days of my life, to behold the beauty of the Lord, and to inquire in his temple" (Psalm 27:4).

The whole key to self-mastery is not to focus on suppressing unwanted desires, but rather to change our focus to striving toward godly desire. In other words, as we grow in prayer and devotion to God, he will give us new and right desires, and he will bring these godly desires to fulfillment. As Psalm 37:4 says, "Take delight in the Lord, and he will give you the desires of your heart."

Temperance does not embrace the pleasures of the culture. Rather, temperance—self-mastery—empowers us to maintain the dignity of the freedom of choice that God has given us, so that we are not enslaved by the lust of the eye, the lust of the flesh, or the pride of life. Through self-mastery, we will not be conformed to the world, but transformed by the renewal of our minds in order to hold to new and right desires (Romans 12:2). Self-mastery is not repression or suppression. Trying to rely on our own strength to guide our fleshly desires is as ineffective as someone putting a wine cork in the very active Kilauea Volcano. Instead, the virtue of temperance is about giving our desires to God and asking him to shape them and make them his own. Through temperance, we are given tremendous freedom to do *God's* will.

CHAPTER TWELVE
HIT THE MARK

I was tandem surfing in waist-high, clean waves south of the pier in Cocoa Beach, Florida, with Amy. It takes trust, commitment, and teamwork to tandem surf well. To show the beauty, grace, and power of the woman joined with the prowess, strength, and protective ability of the man is a rare artistic expression.

She had tandem surfed before with less experienced surfers, but this was the first time for us to surf together. Tandem surfing is an extreme sport, and she had experienced more than her share of bad falls, so she naturally tended to worry about everything that could go wrong instead of focusing on doing it right. When surfing tandem, only one partner can be in charge, and it is the man's responsibility to be the captain of the ship. If two people try to lead or second-guess each other, bad things happen. It's like ballroom dancing; when the partners are really connected, there does not seem to be one person leading and another following even though the man is leading. They move in unison, seamlessly, like they are one person.

She started out well by paddling out quickly, and when we caught a wave, she got up and back to me without wasting time. But then she stiffened, which made it hard for me to surf. Instinct told me that she was trying too hard. More than that, I could sense her trepidation. She was not resting in me or trusting in me and, therefore, could not tune into the physical and verbal signals I gave her.

On the first three waves as we rode down the open face, I called for her to turn in a pirouette and face me, putting her hands in a C-grip on each of my shoulders to prepare to jump into an overhead lift. But Amy could not make the turn. She seemed to be trying, but she was stuck. To complete the moves, I had to muscle her into a turn, and once I even lifted her off the board to unglue her feet from it and get her to turn to face me.

She kept saying, "I am stuck. I can't seem to turn." There was an involuntary resistance to her turn and she couldn't figure out why. Because of all of her previous wipeouts with less experienced partners, she was programmed to be overly cautious, and was constantly watching for danger. As she tried to spin her hips toward me, her eyes fixed straight ahead as if expecting a wipeout. She never took her focus off of what she feared to turn her eyes to me.

Every springboard diver, gymnast, or dancer knows that your body will follow your eyes. Amy was so fearful of falling that she very nearly caused us to wipeout. She was focused on the problem instead of on the solution. When I have a partner in a tandem lift while I am surfing, I can actually sense when her eyes move to look in a direction other than where she is supposed to spot. Without perceptibly even moving her head, simply glancing in another direction will unbalance her. Focus is essential to balance.

I coached her to turn her eyes and her whole head toward me and her hips followed. I told her to let her focus be on me and what I was doing and to tune everything else out. On the next wave, I could sense a huge difference in her energy. She wasn't so stiff. She wasn't trying so hard. She was letting go of control.

We dropped into a wave and I gave her the signal. She turned her eyes and head toward me first, and the rest of her body followed. She executed the turn with perfect ease and then, a moment later, I gave her the signal to jump into the lift. Because she was focused on me, she was able to follow my lead without hesitation. She leaped in perfect timing and easily went into the pose like the rock star I knew she was.

We were ecstatic. She did it perfectly. She kept her eyes on the right spot and she hit her mark. We surfed that wave along the edge of the pier with her friends and family cheering for her, and then she came down gracefully and safely to the board.

Amy had a new understanding of the importance of keeping her focus on the mark. By focusing on her partner, she learned to trust in the signals given to her. Even if she still feared a wipeout, she wasn't focused on that fear, and that gave her the courage and trust she needed to take the leap. The lesson is no different in the virtue of self-mastery. We need to keep our eyes on the mark. We need to keep our eyes on Jesus.

Instead of fighting our disordered desires, all we need to do is refocus our hearts on the mark. Ezekiel 36:26 says, "A new heart I will give you, and a new spirit I will put within you; and I will remove from your body the heart of stone and give you a heart of flesh." In other words, God will give us new desires. The Latin word for *desire* comes from a word meaning the stars or heavenly bodies, which implies a sense of infinity. We need to refocus our gaze to that which is infinite. Let our desires focus on heavenly things.

Both the Hebrew and Greek word for *sin* (*chata'ah* and *harmatia*, respectively) is the same word used for an archer missing the target. Anyone who has ever practiced archery knows how important it is to keep your eye on the bull's-eye. If you look away, you won't make the shot. Likewise, in order to have self-mastery over our passions, we must keep our eye on the target—that is, our desire for intimacy with God. If we focus on the problem or sin, we will miss the mark of holiness. The more we get wrapped up in our weaknesses, or try to suppress disordered passions by our own strength, the more we wipeout.

The Beatitudes are, as the *Catechism* tells us, an example of a God-oriented desire: "The Beatitudes respond to the natural desire for happiness. This desire is of divine origin: God has placed it in the human heart in order to draw man to the One who alone can fulfill it" (CCC 1718). We all desire happiness. Desire is good as long as we place focus on God, who properly orders all of our desires. There is only one way to increase our desire for God, and that is to spend time with him. The Catholic Church has taught us to pray without ceasing. By going to Mass, receiving the sacraments, praying the Liturgy of the Hours, praying the rosary, reading his Word, lectio divina, or using many other treasures the Church has shown us in her bountiful storehouse, we are given ample opportunity to seek God's presence and commune with him.

When I stick to my daily physical regimen of three workouts, I am healthier, more alert, better able to perform my work that day, and always ready for the next surf competition. I am also happier. If I keep my workout routine, my workout routine keeps me. It's the same way with the Liturgy of the Hours. If I keep the Liturgy of the Hours, the Liturgy of the Hours keeps me. I pray the Liturgy of the Hours every sunrise and sunset while down at the beach. This practice is even more important to me than my physical workout routine.

I used to have this deplorable practice. As I did my daily beach workout, I would take a picture of the person with the worst sunburn and post it on social media as the sunburn of the day. Even on a cloudy day an unwise beachgoer can get a bad sunburn. Whether they can see the sun or not, it has an effect on them. In the same way, whether we know it or not, by spending time before the Lord in Eucharistic Adoration, meditating on his Word, or through prayer, a change is taking place in the deepest part of our soul. We are getting a spiritual suntan. When you spend time with God, he is at work in you, changing and ordering your desires. Even when you cannot sense something is happening, the light of Christ is shining on you and transforming you.

People often ask me what they should do to become a better surfer. They are really asking what kind of weightlifting, cardio, or stretching they should practice. I answer them with only one word: *surf!* There is no substitute for time in the water. If you seek self-mastery, there is no substitute for time spent in God's presence. The more I surf, the more I love it and desire to be in the water. The same is true for the time I spend with God. So if you want to live in the virtue of temperance, if you want to have self-mastery over your desires, the best advice I can offer is simply this: Spend time with the Lord and *pray!*

CHAPTER THIRTEEN

THE WAY OF HEROIC VIRTUE: ST. AUGUSTINE

While his mother Monica prayed, Augustine played. In his later years, Augustine confessed that his childhood and younger years were filled with distraction and disordered desires. He let his passions run wild. Temperance was a stranger to him. He had a desire for drinking with his buddies, he had a desire for women, and he had a desire for fame, prestige, and career advancement. In time, he took a mistress. He was faced with many of the same temptations we are today, lured by the empty thrills of sex, drugs, and rock and roll.

Augustine's desires were not limited to the physical world. More and more, his passion for knowledge grew, too. He immersed himself in a cacophony of pagan religion, philosophy, and various Christian heresies that left him unconvinced and confused. As a young man, he left Carthage and hopped a ship to Rome. He deceived his mother into thinking she would be going with him, but told her the wrong time of departure. After a short time in Rome, he headed north to Milan where his prayerful mother joined him. Finally, Augustine found a teacher for whom he had profound respect: Bishop Ambrose.

Soon, what had existed as merely Christian concepts and ideas became the impetus for violence. The emperor joined himself to the Arian heresy that seemed on the verge of dominating Christianity. When Bishop Ambrose became a champion defender of the faith, the emperor sent soldiers to take over the basilica. Augustine witnessed Ambrose risk his life for the God whom he loved and served. Ambrose took a stand inside the basilica along with hundreds of Christians, including Augustine's own mother.

Augustine's life was radically changed. He had seen a different kind of desire and it struck him to the core. These people were not just in love with a concept, they were in love with a very personal God. Augustine fled to a countryside home with several of his philosopher friends, where he found a book about the devotion of Anthony, the monk who gave up his wealth to flee to the desert and pursue intimacy with God.

Augustine wept over his unwillingness to give up the pleasures of the flesh. He wrote, "It was, in fact, my old mistresses, trifles of trifles and vanities of vanities, who still enthralled me. They tugged at my fleshly garments and softly whispered: 'Are you to part with us? And from that moment we will never be with you anymore? And from that moment will not this and that be forbidden you forever?'"[7] He wanted a relationship with God, but was not yet ready to turn over all of his desires.

With a tormenting hurricane of emotions and thoughts flooding his soul, Augustine ran into the garden, out of earshot of his peers. He sobbed, "How long, how long? Tomorrow and tomorrow? Why not now? Why not at this very hour make an end to my uncleanness?"[8]

In response, he heard a child's voice saying, "Pick up and read," and Augustine felt compelled to run into the house and pick up the first thing that he saw to read. It was St. Paul's Letter to the Romans:

> Besides this, you know what hour it is, how it is now the moment for you to wake from sleep. For salvation is nearer to us now than when we became believers; the night is far gone, the day near. Let us then lay aside the

works of darkness and put on the armor of light; let us live honorably as in the day, not in reveling and drunkenness, not in debauchery and licentiousness, not in quarreling and jealousy. (Romans 13:11–13)

Augustine finally surrendered his passions to God. His capacity for passion and desire that had previously missed the mark were now directed toward his creator.

In paintings, Augustine is shown holding a book in one hand and a heart of fire in the other. He turned his focus from the world and cast his eyes on God. The virtue of temperance enabled him to turn the fire of his desires over to God, who ordered them. The work of God in Augustine's heart is evidenced in this prayer:

Late have I loved thee, Beauty so ancient and so new, late have I loved thee. Lo, you were within, but I outside, seeking there for you, and upon the shapely things you have made, I rushed headlong misshapen. You called, shouted, broke through my deafness and flared, blazed, banished my blindness; you lavished your fragrance. I gasped and now I tasted you, and now I hunger and thirst, for you touched me.[9]

Augustine understood that to live in virtue, to live close to God, he must pray. He wrote, "The monks in the desert are said to offer frequent prayers, but these are short and hurled like javelins."[10] He, too, dedicated himself to target practice, hurling his own javelin-like prayers to God. He wrote,

Let's always desire the happy life from the Lord God and always pray for it. But for this reason we turn our mind to the task of prayer at the appointed hour, since that desire grows lukewarm, so to speak, from our involvement in other concerns and occupations. We remind ourselves through the words of prayer to focus our attention on the object of our desire, otherwise, the desire that began to grow lukewarm may grow chill altogether and may totally be extinguished unless it is repeatedly stirred into flame.[11]

We are approaching the deep channel. I look back frequently and can see the relentless lines of surf rising in the distance. If there is a bigger rogue wave coming, it will sneak up on us behind the wall of waves that block my view.

I have no choice. The beleaguered couple's strength is waning and they will not be able to manage another paddle back out if we get caught inside again. If we are going into the impact zone, we need to move through it as quickly as possible. I pull them up next to me.

"This should be fun. We are going to wait for the right moment, and then when I say go, I need for you to hold onto my leash with one hand and paddle as hard as you can with the other. You are going to have the ride of your life. When we get close to the surf, I need for you to do exactly what I say and do it right away. You cannot hesitate because timing is everything."

They look at me with fear and determination in their eyes and nod.

"I am going to have you let go of the leash at some point and paddle with all you've got." I point to the man, "You will go first. I will be behind you and to the left. I will yell for you to paddle and then I will paddle as well. Once you are paddling, don't look back. It will slow you down and might cause the rail of your board to dig and flip you over."

I explain that I will catch the wave behind him and give him a push. This will also allow me to change the angle of his drop if needed.

"Keep paddling until you feel that surge. Then push yourself back a good foot on the board and hang on. Make sure your head is sideways on the board itself so it won't buck up and break your jaw. If you wipeout, go in the fetal position with your hands over your head so you don't get sliced up by

the board or the reef until the wave releases you, then swim away from the dark and toward the light. While you are being held under, just start counting. It may seem like forever, but you will be able to pop up on the surface before you get to thirty. Just stay casual, OK?" I flash a smile.

He grimly looks ahead at the backs of the waves as they break between us and the shore. I feel compelled to warn him against trying to save himself, should he make it through the channel. His previous display of stubborn independence tells me he'll be tempted.

"Ride that wave for several hundred yards. Once it backs off in deeper water, I want you to hold your position until your wife and I get to you. Don't let the current drift you. Hold your position. There is another line of shallow reef between there and the shore. I don't want you to get cut up on it. Besides, I want you to be ready to help your wife if she needs you after I push her into the next wave. You got it?" I probe his eyes, wanting to see what he will do under pressure.

His jaw is set stubbornly, but when he meets my eye, his look turns to determination, "I got it."

I tell his wife to hold her position while I launch her husband into the channel. I assure her I will be back. Her forehead is creased with worry.

"Are we going to be OK?" she asks.

Before I can respond, a baby honu (sea turtle), no bigger than a foot long, pops up its head between us. It floats there with one wing up, letting the wind push it along. It eyes us curiously and pops back down, swimming under her.

The effect of the honu is dramatic. She can't help but smile, a new spark of courage lighting in her eyes.

We wait as the last set rolled past us. It is time.

"Here we go!" I shout.

The

Virtue

of

Fortitude

CHAPTER FOURTEEN

RIP TIDE

My friend Howell and I slipped into the ocean and began to paddle out a quarter of a mile to a surf break called Jocko's, on the north shore of O'ahu. The two of us had surfed epic days together, like riding Rincon on the day the Ventura Pier was destroyed by heavy surf. Despite his vast experience, Howell had never managed conditions like we were facing today. The waves came out of deep water and then suddenly threw out on shallow reef, causing the building surf to break way overhead and the riptide to surge out to sea like a river. We paddled into the rip and, before we knew it, it carried us out into the lineup.

It was bigger than we thought. Swells were running out of the northwest. If we could get in quick and tuck into the hollow wave, we would be able to make a fast run along its face, thereby avoiding the house-size rocks that threatened to rip us to shreds if we did not kick out in time. If we wiped out in front of them, we would have a very bad day.

As the surf kept building, we each rode a few waves. Soon, though, I could see Howell had reached his limit. I had never seen him back down in big surf before, but this was a new spot for him. We liked to say that we always paddle out and we never back down. But this was Hawaii, and the water was heavy. I signaled for him to follow me. It was time to go in.

We paddled into the last wave of a set and surfed down the line into the deeper channel between Jocko's and Laniakea, which was the next break over. As soon as we hit the channel, we were immediately in the grip of that surging riptide that fought us as we tried to make our way back in. We could not win. It pulled us right back out to the lineup every time.

The only way we could get to shore was not to paddle up the current toward the beach, but rather to paddle sideways and cross over the raging rip to the edge of the next break.

We began our paddle across and felt ourselves side slipping out to sea. Paddling hard wasn't going to be enough. We had to read the waves, the reef, and the current and find a course through them with the least resistance. We also had to watch for the razor-sharp coral heads that would disappear under a wave and then, like a sea monster, slowly reappear as the wave passed. If Howell stayed close and followed my course over to the next break, he would be able to avoid the growing danger all around us.

When I finally broke through to the inside of the surf line of the next break and looked back, I saw him in the distance, sitting frozen on his surfboard. The current was sweeping him back toward the peak at Jocko's. If he didn't do something soon, he would either get swept farther out to sea or would have to make a drop in at Jocko's that I knew he was not ready for. His window of opportunity was closing fast.

I paddled all the way back out through the heavy surf and challenged him again to stay close to me. He shook off the fear, lowered his head, and followed me. Still, Howell was not used to such long paddles and he was nearing exhaustion.

"Just one paddle stroke at a time," I called to him.

He kept his head down and kept plowing.

It seemed like an eternity, but it was only a short five minutes before we made it across the rip and over to the inside of the other break. We let the white water roll us toward the beach, where the lazy *honu* fed on the seaweed in the shallows and sunned themselves on the sand, while beachgoers watched their children play.

Having reached safety, Howell was ecstatic. We sat on the sand recovering our breath and looking out to sea. We watched a close-out set that most certainly would have been my friend's doom. We couldn't help but laugh. It was so good to be alive. Howell had portrayed the virtue of fortitude by keeping to the course through the riptide, even though he was frightened. If he hadn't demonstrated this virtue, he might have been killed.

Just like Howell, we must have the courage and fortitude to stay close to God in the heavy waters of our life. Fortitude is the courage to do violence to our own weak will and say no to the easy way, which leads to defeat. Howell courageously left behind the deceptive safety of that deep channel. He had to look fear in the face and say, "Not today, fear. You are not going to dominate me." Even when fear threatens to overwhelm us, or when our enemies set up camp around us, we must trust in God. Like David, we must "fear no evil, for you are with me" (Psalm 23:4). That kind of trust takes fortitude.

The *Catechism* teaches us that:

> Fortitude is the moral virtue that ensures firmness in difficulties and constancy in the pursuit of the good. It strengthens the resolve to resist temptations and to overcome obstacles in the moral life. The virtue of fortitude enables one to conquer fear, even fear of death, and to face trials and persecutions. It disposes one even to renounce and sacrifice his life in defense of a just cause. (CCC 1808)

Fortitude is the determined pursuit of the good. Fear can be like a big shadow on the wall that is really only a projection of a little toy sitting on the countertop next to a lamp. How can there be any fear when we are with God? God is love, and perfect love casts out fear. His perfect love reveals the toy for what it is, and wipes the shadow of fear from our hearts. I know that, whether I live or die or push forward in prolonged suffering, God is with me.

God knows how susceptible we are to fear. Time and again, he offers us comfort in his Word. Even glancing at the book of Psalms gives us numerous verses of comfort:

> The LORD is my light and my salvation;
> whom shall I fear?
> The LORD is the stronghold of my life;
> of whom shall I be afraid? (Psalm 27:1)

> Be strong, and let your heart take courage,
> all you who wait for the LORD. (Psalm 31:24)

> I sought the LORD, and he answered me,
> and delivered me from all my fears. (Psalm 34:4)

No matter what life brings, God is with us. When we are afraid, we can say with confidence, "I will stand in the Lord's will and put my trust in him alone." My motto for my first Ninja Black Belt was a paraphrase of Psalm 61:2 by the warrior-poet, King David: "Lead me to the rock too high to climb and I will climb it."

As the *Catechism* explains, fortitude isn't just about overcoming fear. It is also about firmness, consistency, and resolve. To have fortitude means to dedicate yourself to something, no matter the obstacle. Because of this, it is natural to talk about fortitude in the context of athletics. Every year, I take on a new physical challenge that requires fortitude. We can develop fortitude in situations like distance paddling, or training for a Spartan race, or pushing our limits in bigger surf. Through an athlete's physical dedication, we can see a metaphor for our spiritual life as well. Fortitude prepares us for the times in life when we must stand up for what is right, for what is just, with the resolve to never back down. Fortitude is like a fullback who keeps his head down and runs over the opposition. Fortitude understands there is a job to be done, a goal to accomplish, and sets its sights on it without distraction. Even in the face of suffering, fortitude allows us to maintain our focus on what really matters.

When I think back to the economic collapse in 2008, I remember that it could not have happened at a worse time for me and my children. My four children were coming of age and were in various stages of being launched into their lives, which meant college bills and a lot of other expenses. Negative cash flow built up, and I soon ran through all my investments.

At the time, it was perplexing. Here I was, a businessman and financial professional. I still lived in a nice home, had a nice car, and provided for my family, but during the downturn I'd sometimes see a homeless man on the street who had more in his beggar's cup than I had in my bank account. Despite years of financial security, I suddenly found myself scratching for every nickel and dime. To outsiders, my life looked comfortable, even luxurious. But my inner reality was very different. My lack of prudence in financial decisions had wrought very real consequences.

By the grace of God, what I lacked in prudence I made up for in fortitude. Despite the apparent hopelessness of my situation, I knew that God was bigger than my fears. I rose early every morning and worked harder than I ever had in my life to make up for my bad investments. Life had taught me that all I had to do was keep going. I kept my head down and pulled the plow. God was with me, and I kept pulling and pulling until I made it through to the other side.

Something beautiful happened during that dark time. I began to notice the smaller blessings in life, like the wind whispering in the palm trees above me, and the shimmering waves at sunrise that promised a new day was coming. I started to go to daily Mass and became more consistent in my prayer life. Even in the darkest valley, God was waiting for me.

At that time in my life I experienced in a new way what St. Paul said in his Letter to the Philippians, "I know what it is to have little, and I know what it is to have plenty. In any and all circumstances I have learned the secret of being well-fed and of going hungry, of having plenty and of being in need" (Philippians 4:12).

Even as my bank account shrank, I drank deeply from the treasury of riches of the two-thousand-year tradition of the Church. I found the writings of the early Church Fathers and discovered Mother Angelica on EWTN. I was intrigued by this folksy nun who spoke in common language about the deep mysteries of God. EWTN's teaching was true to the magisterium of the Church, and I found a profound depth in all I was learning. In the midst of the crashing waves, I—like the disciples in the boat—encountered the peace and assurance of Christ.

Jesus said, "In the world you face persecution. But take courage, I have conquered the world" (John 16:33). What do we have to fear in the middle of this valley of the shadow of death? Nothing! He has even prepared a table for us in the presence of our enemies (see Psalm 23). He is our strength and shield (see Psalm 28). He even gives us a song when our hearts are troubled: "By day the Lord commands his steadfast love, and at night his song is with me, a prayer to the God of my life" (Psalm 42:8). Paul and Silas understood this verse better than anyone, perhaps. Even in prison, they sang hymns of praise to God.

God does not abandon us in our suffering, no matter what our suffering may be. Just as he was with Paul and Silas in prison, he is with you in the prison of your fear. You may feel overcome by the world, but remember that Christ is in you, and he has already conquered the world. The virtue of fortitude will bear you through the deep channel amid the crashing surf. Remember, our response to suffering opens our heart to a depth of communion with God that is impossible without it.

How's this for perspective? "St. Teresa of Avila said that the most miserable earthly life, seen from the perspective of heaven, looks like one night in an inconvenient hotel."[12] Our life on earth is just a day and a night before we enter eternity. This is the hope that fuels our fortitude.

No matter what we face, we know that this life is temporary, and that Christ came to earth and shared in our suffering that we might be with him in heaven. Let us wait with Jesus in the garden of Gethsemane for this one hour that we have on earth. I am not trying to diminish the difficulty of life. Jesus's suffering and our suffering are very real. But so, too, is the reality of a heavenly home in the presence of God. Remember, "What no eye has seen, nor ear heard, nor the human heart conceived, what God has prepared for those who love him" (1 Corinthians 2:9). We must not be distracted by the shadow suffering casts on the wall, for it is our path to our eternity with God that is so much greater than our present reality.

CHAPTER FIFTEEN
STORM CHASER

ere's an idea: If you want to have a lot of fun and develop the virtue of fortitude, why not pedal your bicycle across the United States, from San Diego, California, to Jacksonville, Florida? If you go in May, like I did, you might get lucky and have eight days of record-breaking heat along the way. Nothing develops fortitude like blazing sun and the open road.

When you invite your daughter to drive the escort vehicle, encourage her to become a vegan just before the trip (you can imagine how this endeared her to the beef-loving Texans). It also helps if she staves off terminal boredom by spending hours each day talking on the cell phone in the middle of the desert, where the deer, antelope, and AT&T roam. What brings a parent more opportunity for fortitude than maxed-out roaming charges?

After a light workout pedaling hundreds of miles over the Rocky Mountains, try flipping your bicycle end-over-end in west Texas. That is quite a conversation starter with the road construction crews! Continue pedaling for two full days through thousands of grasshoppers the size of frogs. Between the unending melody of squishing bugs and the splatter that will cover you in organic goo, you're bound to find enlightenment. Then, after not seeing water for nearly ten days, become an amateur storm chaser and pedal directly into a tropical storm. It was a six-day onslaught of howling wind, rain, lightning—and, oh, did I mention wind?

Of course, no adventure in fortitude would be complete without so-called "luxury" motels with broken televisions and vibra-beds, without a functioning Jacuzzi to soothe your

THE VIRTUE OF FORTITUDE

sore muscles. The water in the pools will always be a strange, glowing color, and the smoke-free room is guaranteed to reek of Marlboros. It's just part of the charm.

The next morning from the comfort of your narrow, painful bicycle seat, you too can discover that dried-out animal carcasses have a mesquite fragrance in the desert, while the humidity of Louisiana gives the smell of skunk a particular and profound pungency. Even carcass-free roads provide ample opportunity to embrace fortitude when fun-loving truckers honk their sonorous horns at you and their draft blows you side-saddle on your bike.

People would often ask me along the way, "Why? Why would you endeavor to take such an incredible journey?"

You want to know why? I'll tell you.

The truth is that I learned a great deal about fortitude over the course of those twenty-five hundred miles. My daughter, Fawn, and I started with a vision, developed a plan, and ultimately proved our ability to stay the course, no matter what the odds. The reward for that adventure was not just at the end, when we pedaled onto the sandy beaches of Florida and dove into the cool waters of the Atlantic. It came moment by moment, mile by mile. We knew we were accomplishing something special. Not only were we raising money for my friend's lupus treatment, we were also growing in respect for each other as we worked together to accomplish what seemed like an insurmountable goal.

By keeping our eyes on the Lord and on our goal, every breath became a prayer for God to provide us with his power, grace, and endurance. At first we tested our limits, then we pushed our limits, and finally we broke through our limits. Even when my daughter had had enough and wanted to quit, she stuck with it, knowing I could not complete my journey without her. In the most difficult moments, love for me fueled her fortitude.

The virtue of fortitude has an accumulative effect on the quality of our life. When we build it into the foundation of our lives, it begins to build us, providing strength we never knew we had. Getting up one hour earlier to have prayer time, staying on task in work or studies another ten minutes, or seeing a task to completion constructs a solidity in our soul. The sheer act of sticking with it, of seeing something through, reveals triumphs of the heart and mind that have a lasting impact. It is exciting, really, to see each mile-marker pass and know that we are accomplishing something God set before us. It is fortitude that guides us toward our goal of hearing God say, "Well done, good and trustworthy slave" (Matthew 25:21).

Do you want to have a sense of fulfillment in your life? Choose to serve God and his people, and you will undoubtedly know fulfillment. Servanthood is one of the defining characteristics of Christ's ministry. He surprised those who followed him by washing their feet in an act of service. Sharing God's love in such an intimate and humble way was life-giving, not only to Jesus, but to those to whom he ministered. Likewise, the pope refers to himself as the servant of the servants of God. We are called to "the least of these," and by answering that call in service, we find fulfillment (Matthew 25:40). I think of responsibility as using our *ability* in *response* to need. God gives us responsibility to those he loves, and he promises that "my yoke is easy, and my burden is light" (Matthew 11:30). He has uniquely gifted you with abilities and desires for the cause that he has for you. Responding to him in fortitude promises great satisfaction.

So many in our age are busy seeking instant gratification, but they neglect the words of Jesus. He spoke clearly when he said, "Those who try to make their life secure will lose it, but who lose their life will keep it" (Luke 17:33). The only true satisfaction we can find is in Christ, who said, "I am the bread of life. Whoever comes to me will never be hungry, and whoever believes in me will never be thirsty" (John 6:35). What, then, should we set our sights on but God? The virtue of fortitude promises to lead us into his provision and fulfillment by guiding us more deeply into his love.

There is a sacredness in diligently pursuing our work and our goals in the virtue of fortitude. Fortitude is the necessary virtue to accomplish work. Adam was given work—to tend the garden and bring forth springs. King David worked among the sheep, and Jesus worked with his hands as a carpenter. Jesus could have been born into a wealthy home, but instead he was born into a working-class home. His father was an artisan. Jesus knew the weight and feel of wood and for what purpose each piece of wood and tool could be used. He had the fortitude and patience to saw, carve, and bore through raw lumber in order to create useful and even beautiful items. At the end of each day, as he brushed the wood shavings off his arms, Jesus understood the sacredness and satisfaction of work and the virtue of fortitude that it took to be productive. The fortitude he learned in his early years of working fortified him for ministry. Fortitude prepared him for his calling.

When we are young and pursuing our education or working in a job that we can't stand, we need to see it as a necessary part of acquiring skills for our long-term goals. The fortitude we practice now prepares us for our calling, growing in us a quiet strength that we don't even know we have until we need it. By accumulating daily acts of fortitude—whether in work, family life, or our relationship with God—we build the character we need to accomplish something bigger than ourselves.

I recently visited my alma mater, Baylor University, for the first time in decades. I showed my son where I studied, worked, and lived. I remember working at a CPA firm during the afternoon, waiting tables at a Greek restaurant a few nights a week, and handling baggage at the small airport on the weekends. While most of the others seemed to be pledging fraternities or partying on the weekend, I worked and studied. Looking back, I can now attribute my fortitude to my hopes for a wife and family. I had dreams and goals, but being a husband and father were the most important to me. I can look at my life now in absolute gratefulness for the young man I was then and for the fortitude God instilled in me during those early years.

There is great joy in having a sense of purpose in our life. God has wired us to tend to our vineyard, water our garden, and to move mountains in pursuit of his will. We long to hear our Lord tell us, "Well done, good and faithful servant." Through the virtues, he has given us the tools we need to accomplish his calling. If, like Jesus, we are diligent in the work at hand, carving and smoothing rough lumber into useful and beautiful items, then God will build us up in forti- tude. Even when the smell of desert road kill fills our nostrils and our legs and back burn beneath the sun, fortitude will carry us on, mile by mile, to the completion of our goal and the satisfaction of a job well done. It should be our prayer that, like St. Paul, we will one day be able to say in confi- dence, "I have fought the good fight, I have finished the race, I have kept the faith" (2 Timothy 4:7). If we allow prudence to be the charioteer and fortitude to be the horse pulling the chariot, we will be amazed by where God leads us. We will be amazed at what we accomplish and what vistas we see.

CHAPTER SIXTEEN

THE WAY OF HEROIC VIRTUE: BLESSED JOSE LUIS SANCHEZ DEL RIO

In the 1920s, the Mexican government banned religion and began exiling Catholic priests and seizing Church property. In time, the persecution became bloody. Young Jose Luis Sanchez del Rio watched as his older brothers joined the rebel army, the *Cristeros*. Like the young King David, he was not allowed to go to battle because of his youth. Jose begged the general to let him serve and insisted he was more than willing to give his life for the cause of Christ. The general finally relented and the young boy was given a horse to ride as he carried the flag for his troops.

Holding the flag was an important role. During the confusion of battle, troops can easily become disoriented. Through the noise and smoke, they may lose track of the direction of their regiment. The flag, held high above the battle, becomes their rallying point. The men admired Jose and soon gave him the nickname, St. Tarcisius, an early Christian saint who was martyred while protecting the Eucharist from desecration. Jose was not only carrying the flag of the troops, he was raising the banner of Christ as well. With courage and determined love for God, the men of the Mexican resistance battled to retain their religious freedom.

During a heavy battle, the fighting grew close to the general and his horse was killed. Jose gave the reigns of his own horse to him. As the man returned to battle, the boy held his ground. He used up his ammunition and was soon captured and thrown into the local sacristy—ironically, the place where he had dreamed of serving as a priest one day.

The army tortured Jose and another boy, ordering them to renounce Christ, but they refused. Jose watched his friend hanged, but his fortitude was not shaken.

"I will join you soon in heaven," Jose told his dying friend.

When the angry soldiers ordered him to say, "Death to Christ the King," Jose instead yelled, "*Viva Cristo Rey!*" ("Long live Christ the King!"). Enraged, they took their machetes and flayed the soles of his feet, then forced him to walk the long way around the village to the cemetery where he would be killed and buried. Despite his suffering, he continued as they hacked at him with their machetes, yelling at him to renounce Christ.

"*Viva Cristo Rey!*" he shouted again.

The soldiers stabbed at him with their bayonets, but still, the boy did not relent. Finally, the commander pulled out his pistol and shot him. Jose fell face down on the ground. For a moment, the soldiers thought he was dead. But then he reached out and traced a cross in the blood-soaked earth. To their utter amazement, Jose lifted his head one more time, pulled himself forward, kissed the cross, and died.

Jose Luis Sanchez del Rio was only fourteen when he died at the hands of enraged soldiers. Those who witnessed the event were horrified by the brutality of his death, but the boy's incredible fortitude left an even deeper impression on the world. His martyrdom, like so many, was violent and tragic, but his faith and his refusal to deny the truth of Christ continues to inspire generations of Catholics. He carries the flag and shows us the way. His final, agonizing moments demonstrate the remarkable fortitude of a hero, and like him, we must continue to call out, "*I will never give in! Viva Cristo Rey!*"

The set of waves is almost upon us. I know this is our shot, and hope my companions have listened well to my instructions.

"Here we go!" I repeat. I call to him, "Remember, once you start to really drop in, I need for you to quickly scoot back a whole foot on the board, OK?"

His knuckles are white as he grips the edge of his board. "Got it."

My instructions will position him just far enough forward so that his weight on the back of his board will not plow and slow him down in the water. If he paddles too slowly, the wave might pick him up and throw him like a toy into the pit fifteen feet below him. However, if he is too far forward, he will bury the nose of the board into the water as he makes his drop, something surfers call pearling because it is like digging for oysters. I already know he will not have the stamina to survive either type of wipeout.

"Keep your paddle on the board next to you. Paddle as hard as you can. Once you feel full acceleration, hang on."

I want to get him into the first and smaller wave, which is approaching fast. I can see this is a bigger set than I had hoped for, but we need to go.

I turn to her. "Can you paddle out to sea about thirty yards and stay there?"

She is nervous, but the courage instilled by her encounter with the little honu *is still fresh. With a nod, she begins to paddle out.*

I wait a few more seconds as the wave approaches and yell at him, "PADDLE!"

Panicked, he thrashes his arms wildly in an effort to pick up speed. The wave looms up behind, casting its shadow and sucking me back toward it. Within moments, he is where I need him to be, so I start my paddle. I power as hard I can and yell to him over the roar of the ocean with each breath, "Paddle!" People tend to stop paddling when they feel the wave lift them, but that is when they need to paddle the hardest.

He hesitates for a moment and looks back, skipping a paddle stroke with one hand. Dread contorts his face when he sees the size of the wave behind him.

"Keep paddling!" I command.

I am sliding down the face of the wave toward him with my arm extended. I grab the tail of his board and angle it slightly to the left, pushing with all my might. As soon as he is out of my grip, I pull back on my board and sit back so I will not catch the wave. He is on his own.

"HANG ON!" I shout over the avalanche of water.

I hear him scream as he disappears on the other side of the wave.

The

Virtue

of

Faith

CHAPTER SEVENTEEN

THE ANCIENT PATH

One of my heroes of the faith is the cigar aficionado, and atheist-turned-Catholic G.K. Chesterton. He contrasted the "rational" or "sad" virtues of justice, temperance, prudence, and fortitude with the "exuberant" (even "unreasonable") virtues of faith, hope, and love. He wrote:

> The Christian virtues of faith, hope, and charity are in their essence as unreasonable as they can be.... Charity means pardoning what is unpardonable, or it is no virtue at all. Hope means hoping when things are hopeless, or it is no virtue at all. And faith means believing the incredible, or it is no virtue at all.[13]

Chesterton opined that justice, prudence, self-mastery, and fortitude are all about restraint, moderation, and duty. Living a life based on these qualities involves discipline instead of freedom. On the other hand, he thought of the three theological virtues of faith, hope, and love as the "fun" virtues. With these, there's no holding back—you just go for it. No need for moderation or restraint here. You can never have enough faith, hope, and love.

Chesterton enjoyed paradoxes, and he certainly saw them in the three theological virtues. We're to have faith in the unseen, believing in a God who can't be measured by our physical eyes or minds. We are to love the unlovable and maintain hope in hopeless situations. To the world, the thought of clinging to these paradoxes seems crazy. But Chesterton saw these virtues as a vehicle through which we can "have life, and have it more abundantly" (John 10:10).

The *Catechism* says, "The human virtues are rooted in the theological virtues, which adapt man's faculties for participation in the divine nature: for the theological virtues relate directly to God. They dispose Christians to live in a relationship with the Holy Trinity. They have the One and Triune God for their origin, motive, and object" (*CCC* 1812). Infused with the theological virtues, the four human virtues draw us into greater intimacy with God.

So we start our journey into the three theological virtues by looking first at faith. Our faith is the cornerstone of our spiritual lives. Without it, we are lost at sea, vulnerable to every changing tide and strong current. The Word of God tells us over and over that the Lord is near the faithful, no matter what. Jesus says incredible things about the power of faith in Mark 11:22–23: "Have faith in God. Truly I tell you, if you say to this mountain, 'Be taken up and thrown into the sea,' and if you do not doubt in your heart, but believe that what you say will come to pass, it will be done for you." Faith can literally move mountains, part seas, and set us free.

Not long ago, I headed out for my beach workout. I walked the mile and a half to the other end of Waikiki Beach near the harbor entrance. I had walked to the same spot nearly every day for more than a decade, but that day something hidden and secret was awaiting me.

The ocean floor is rough in this area, and it is tough to work your way through the broken lava rock and coral fragments to get to the deeper water. Navigating this path is more challenging than walking barefoot through a dark living room strewn with Legos. Surfers and paddlers tread carefully here to get through the shallows so they can paddle out.

As I was making my way, an older paddler stepped off his one-man outrigger canoe. Flipping it up on his shoulder, he easily strolled right out of the water without looking down or wincing in pain.

"How was the paddle?" I asked.

He responded with the glow of mastery. "It was good. I paddled up to Diamond Head and back."

I couldn't help but admire his unflinching walk across the jagged terrain. Looking down at his feet, the very low tide allowed me to notice something. All of the stones, shells, and broken coral had been cleared in a one-foot-wide ancient path in the ocean floor that had been smoothed out by centuries of flowing water. This narrow but easy path led directly out into the deeper water.

So it is with our faith. Why tiptoe our way around, flirting with the latest pop-theology, self-appointed spiritual guru, or moral trend? Why not follow the well-worn ancient path that the great masters of our faith followed before us?

In the Catholic faith, we hold the Scriptures in one hand and the *Catechism* in the other. The *Catechism* is based upon the written and oral tradition of the Church, passed down from Christ and the apostles and their successors, to help us properly and more deeply understand the Bible. The Church has provided the *Catechism* so that we can more easily seek God's reason and revelation. We can read the writings of Athanasius, Jerome, Augustine, Irenaeus, Aquinas, and Teresa of Avila, just to name a few. The insights of Scripture and the *Catechism* flow like water over rough stone. They have carved a path for us, smooth and narrow, that leads us to the deep waters.

When someone asked Jesus, "What must a man do to be saved?" Jesus responded, "Have faith in God" (Mark 11:22). For centuries, the faith of those who have gone before us has smoothed away the rough edges by asking questions, seeking answers, and meditating on the revealed knowledge of God.

Theirs was an active faith, both in works and in seeking under-standing. The example of these heroes—the saints, the great Catholic writers and thinkers, and of course, the example of Christ—all lead us down the ancient, narrow, and true path, taking us ever deeper into the wild and untamable adventure of God's love.

CHAPTER EIGHTEEN

FAITH LEAPS

I walked out onto the tarmac with my son, Jeremiah. The noise of the twin-engine prop plane was deafening, and the tail wash from the propellers kept pushing us as we tried to enter the door behind the wing. We climbed in with a dozen other jumpers.

As the plane climbed to twelve thousand feet, it began to turn in long circles. About halfway to our jump altitude, the jump master who was sitting next to the exit door casually slid it open, then leaned against the wall and continued reading a book. My son looked at the open door and the instructor, who seemed like he could fall out at any minute, and then looked over at me with a worried expression. I gave him the thumbs up and he grinned, flashing it back to me. Then I nodded to the guy sitting a little in front and across from my son.

The man was a first-time jumper and had a look of absolute terror. He sat in front of the instructor whom he was attached to for the tandem jump. The nervous jumper kept looking down at his gear, checking and rechecking it. Jumping out of an airplane takes guts. I am always scared before I jump. But I had never seen anyone so freaked out.

As we finally flew over the jump site, the plane started to empty out as one tandem team at a time disappeared out the door. Finally there were just two tandem teams and me, a solo jumper, left. It's an eerie feeling to be one of the last people in what was a crowded plane just a minute ago. Jeremiah and I were purposefully positioned to be the last ones out because I wanted to jump after him and hang out close to him once our canopies opened.

I could see the look of anxiety and excitement grow on my son's face. There was just one team in front of us and then we would go. The other first-time jumper was ghostly pale. Suddenly, his jump master signaled for Jeremiah and I to pass him. As we squeezed by, I understood why. A horrible smell told us he had lost control of his bowels. Even with the door of the plane wide open, the stench filled the plane. I did not envy his jump master as Jeremiah and I launched ourselves out into fresh, open air.

Jeremiah leaped and then I followed as we dropped at up to 120 miles an hour from twelve thousand feet to six thousand feet; as our canopies opened I finally caught up to my son and was able to shout to him the traditional Hawaiian saying, "Hang loose!" He waved at me with a victory salute.

The man back in the plane had taken the full jump course, just like everyone else. He understood all about parachute technology. He was even tethered to an experienced skydiver who would ensure his safety. Still, he could not take the leap. The jumper had knowledge, but he lacked faith; and *faith* is the only thing that could have gotten him out of that plane.

In skydiving and in life, fear is natural. But, no matter how much fear a skydiver may show before he jumps the first time, usually the moment he leaps, a great exultation lights up his face. Having the faith to leap out of the safety of the plane rewards skydivers with an incredible view and a remarkable experience, not to mention a killer burst of adrenaline and a feeling that you can conquer the world.

Every time I jump out of a plane, I feel the same rush that I feel when I take a leap of faith in response to God. Jesus challenged Peter to exercise his faith and to step out of the boat. Even now, he challenges us to take the leap of faith and truly follow him.

Whether it's jumping out of planes, or out of boats, or embarking on some other equally breathtaking venture, faith, by its very nature, means *action*. Faith is dynamic, like pent-up energy wanting to explode. Faith without action is dead. Even the thief on the cross next to Jesus took action. His faith compelled him to ask, "Jesus, remember me when you come into your kingdom" (Luke 23:42). He saw the truth of who Christ was and took a leap.

Does your faith go beyond the malaise of a casual acknowledgment of God's existence and a casual prayer life? Does it compel you to *leap*? There is an easy way to answer this question. Look at your life. If your faith is one of action, your life will naturally reflect Christ. Your life will be filled with the greatest adventure of all—going deep into intimacy with God and responding to the heartbeat of his moment-by-moment guidance in your life. You see, faith and deeds go hand in hand. As James reminds us, "So faith by itself, if it has no works, is dead" (James 2:17). The virtue of faith, as we know, seeks understanding. But it also turns your life into one of action.

There is the initial leap of faith that is simply believing that all God says is true. But there's more to it than that. God is calling you to continually *move out* in faith. He is calling you to do the impossible, every day. God is not calling us to a life of mediocrity. He doesn't want us to be full of knowledge but refuse to jump out of the plane. We can't let lack of faith stink the place up. He is calling each of us to be a saint. He is calling each of us to walk the way of heroic virtue.

The ancient way of the hero is one of perseverance and dedication, no matter what trials may come. A hero's faith does not doubt, for "the doubter, being double-minded and unstable in every way, must not expect to receive anything from the Lord" (James 1:8). God does not want us to waiver in our faith. Faith establishes in us a firmness in the knowledge of God, and a trust in him.

A hero's faith is active in the present moment, and does not put things off. The Bible tells us that "now is the acceptable time; see, now is the day of salvation" (2 Corinthians 6:2). The urgency to the question of faith in Jesus is as real as the ground coming up at a skydiver at 120 miles an hour. We are all moving at terminal velocity through life. We have only one parachute, and that is faith in Jesus.

After our death, we won't need faith. Whether we are in heaven or in hell, the time for faith will have passed. We know for certain that God respects the dignity as well as the perilousness of our free will, for he will let us have for eternity exactly what we loved, clung to, and put our faith in while on earth. We either cling to Jesus or refuse Jesus, both here and in eternity.

God gives each of us a gift of faith. In 1 Corinthians 12:9, Paul says that the Holy Spirit gives us this gift. God breathes it into each of us. Your vibrant, living faith is your parachute. Even in times when what we are being asked to do seems impossible, the virtue of faith enables us to leap. God is full of surprises. Along the path of your life, there will be times when Jesus looks at you with a wink and says, "Come on. I have an adventure planned for you." God may be calling you to take a leap of faith and help start a Catholic radio station or get married or start a new career. Whatever it is he is asking, remember you are not jumping alone. He is with you.

CHAPTER NINETEEN

FAITH RESTS

I patrolled the winding road down into the early morning fog that enveloped me as I drove toward the coast. Every day for six consecutive weeks, I had strapped my longboard on my car and headed for the surf spot that was made famous by The Beach Boys—Ventura County Line.

I climbed down the ten-foot-high cliff to the cold sand, set up my beach chair, angled my surfboard on its side to provide a little bit of protection from the wind, and draped my wetsuit that was still wet from the day before over a big boulder, hoping the sun would eventually burn through and dry it before I paddled out. In the meantime, my coffee kept me warm enough.

I sat down and opened the pages of my dog-eared Bible to continue reading where I had left off the day before. That summer, in between surf sessions, I sat huddled against the morning cold as I read through the entire Bible in six weeks. In fact, I read all of the New Testament, all of the Old Testament, and then all of the New Testament again. In that high-speed viewing of the Scripture, I was able to perceive powerful and intricate themes that were woven through like the threads of those tapestries hanging in the Vatican Museums.

One of the threads I noticed was running through the whole tapestry like a vein of pure gold. It was the invitation to enter into God's rest. I saw verse after verse offer the promise of rest in God. And, as Hebrews 4:1 says, "While the promise of entering his rest is still open, let us take care of you that none of you should seem to have failed to reach it."

I did not want to fail to reach his rest. I wanted, as the Letter to the Hebrews exhorts, to "make every effort to enter" it (Hebrews 4:11).

It seems somewhat paradoxical that we need to work at resting. When my son Shane was young, he was a ball of energy. He was always on the move. When I tried to hold him and cuddle with him, he would squirm and wriggle until he was free to run and play again. Sometimes, I think we are like this with God. We are so busy with our own plans and agendas that we have no interest in rest, and so we lose a certain opportunity for intimacy with him.

Rest is not a mere request from God. Rest is so important to him that he commanded the Israelites to observe the Sabbath—one day of rest each week. In addition, every seven years was to be a *year* of rest. "Be still, and know that I am God" is an invitation to recline our soul, to cease our relentless striving, and to incline our ear to his heart in trust and intimacy (Psalm 46:10).

Jesus teaches us to rest in the midst of adversity. He teaches us peace in the midst of the storm, for he is our safe harbor. Remember the story of Jesus sleeping in the back of the boat while his disciples freaked out about the weather? When they woke him because they feared they were about to die, he asked them a sobering question, "And he said to them, 'Why are you afraid, you of little faith?' Then he got up and rebuked the winds and the sea; and there was a dead calm" (Matthew 8:26). Their inability to rest in the storm was a reflection of their small faith. The disciples had not yet realized that walking with Christ meant that, not only had their lives changed, but their paradigm had changed as well. They had entered into the Kingdom of God; they had entered into Christ's rest.

Our culture seems to think that worry is a virtue. (Maybe you're worried that God left worry off the list of virtues.) Valid concern and prudence is one thing, but taking on a concern that we can do nothing about accomplishes nothing.

It prevents us from praising God and resting in him. Worry takes the fun and joy out of life. Worry is a party crasher who, when allowed in, becomes a party pooper; but praise and thankfulness are the bouncers at the door who won't let him in.

Worry can consume us. Worry is a lack of faith. St. Paul tells us, "Do not worry about anything, but in everything by prayer and supplication with thanksgiving let your requests be made known to God" (Philippians 4:6). Constant worry can corrode our hearts, but God instructs us: "Keep your heart with all vigilance, for from it flow the springs of life" (Proverbs 4:23). The sin of worry denies the very nature of God, forgetting that he is "our refuge and strength, a very present help in trouble" (Psalm 46:1).

Faith rests. We are to be like the bride in Song of Solomon who comes up from the wilderness "leaning upon her beloved" (8:5). God is so trustworthy, so strong, so mighty that we can lean fully on him. Have you ever seen a toddler sound asleep on her father's shoulder in the midst of a bustling crowd? *That* is faith. That is true rest. The child's trust for her father is so complete that she can abandon herself to his will—believing that he will deliver her safely, no matter how busy or loud the crowd around her. She can lean her head on his shoulder and rest.

Are you able to rest in God's will completely? God's perfect will, which is the same as his perfect love, offers us refuge in every storm. If we abide in him, there is no need to strive or worry for anything. When we worry, we are actually trying to exert our will over his. Making anything other than God and His will our goal is ultimately idolatry. Only God brings the fulfillment of rest. There is an infinite thirst in us that can only be satisfied by our union with the infinite God.

Jesus teaches us rest in the midst of a storm. Did you catch that? He does not challenge us to cross over into the land of rest at low tide and small surf. Like the disciples, we cross over when the tide is high and the wind is pitching our boat. It doesn't take much faith to cross glassy, calm waters. But in the storm, when the temptation hits to wake Jesus because we think he is not aware of our needs, God reminds us to be still, to trust, and to rest in the knowledge that he is God. The virtue of faith is not white-knuckled. It is not clinging to the side of the boat, screaming and pleading for Jesus to wake up.

David reminds us, "You prepare a table before me in the presence of my enemies" (Psalm 23:5). I can just picture arrows flying and commanders shouting orders from their thundering chariots while Jesus is whistling and setting a table for afternoon tea. This verse always reminds me of the unique poker game that is played at rodeos. Four or five cowboys sit around a table in the middle of the corral, casually chewing tobacco and playing poker while an angry bull snorts and stamps its hooves, glaring at them. (When one of the cowboys wants another card and says, "Hit me," he hopes the bull doesn't take him literally.) The cowboys' job is to be the last one seated as the bull charges at them. If a cowboy jumps to safety, he is eliminated.

Faith, however, is not foolhardiness. It isn't about deliberately putting oneself in harm's way and expecting God to bail us out. Rather, faith is the casual confidence that we can develop in God as we walk the ancient path. Faith is not saying, "If I just try hard enough to believe, God will answer my prayer, and I'll get what I want." At its best, that is just faith in faith, not faith in God. The virtue of faith is a toddler sleeping on her father's shoulder. It is resting in God's fidelity.

When my tandem partner tries too hard, we fall. I always tell her, "Don't try *hard*. Try *easy*." When she is at rest—in other words, when she has faith in me as a partner—she can more easily flow with me and sense my intentions. If she tenses up and tries too hard, I know there is no way we can carve through the water and hit our lifts, and I'm forced to kick out of the wave. But when she is tuned into me, our movements become fluid and strong.

When our faith rests in God, God is able to work with us. When we work by our own efforts, God folds his arms and watches us, waiting for us to wear ourselves out so that he can lift, lead, and move us. When we work, God rests. When we rest, God works. By leaning on him, our hearts are strengthened and we can be still. "Try easy" doesn't mean *not* trying. It means trusting. It means letting go of our worry and resting in the arms of our Father. As you seek to flow in God's will and power, don't cling to the side of the boat with white-knuckled worry. Don't try too hard. Trust. Rest. And *try easy*.

CHAPTER TWENTY

FAITH MOVES MOUNTAINS

I raised Krystl Apeles high over my head in a victory lift on the Waikiki beach podium in front of the statue of my boyhood hero, Duke Kahanamoku. We had received our first International Surfing Association (ISA) World Masters Tandem Surfing Trophy. As the cameras rolled and the crowd applauded, I had only one thought: "Whenever I am weak, then I am strong" (2 Corinthians 12:10). This verse pulsed through my mind and heart in the exhilaration of the moment. You see, there was a time when I was plagued by debilitating back pain.

My back had been in constant spasm for nearly fifteen years. I would spend weeks at a time in bed, unable to function. The pain made me edgy, had drained me emotionally, and restricted my physical activity. The cold water of a California surf session would soothe it, but by the time I got home, I was walking with my back crooked over to one side again. I was living in a prison of pain.

I had been to several doctors and therapists and even a committee of the best back specialists and researchers in the world at University of California Los Angeles. But they could not determine what was causing my pain and had no recommendation for treatment. Physical therapy hadn't helped; in fact, it had almost crippled me. I had accepted that I would live with the pain for the rest of my life—unless God chose to heal me.

I knew God could heal me if he wanted to, but like St. Paul, who suffered a thorn in his flesh his whole life, I also knew my pain was being allowed by God for a higher purpose (2 Corinthians 12:7). The pain did keep me humble and dependent on him. Yet, I prayed almost every moment for relief, and I had been prayed for many times.

When we pray for guidance, intercession for others, provision, healing, and miracles, we must pray believing that God will move in accordance with his will. God is not a vending machine. We don't just blab it and grab it. We don't just name it and claim it. We don't will it by faith into manifesting. We trust in God to lead us in the proper way to pray; and we pray with faith—not presumption. We don't always get the exact results that we wish for, but our prayers are always heard and always answered in the way God chooses in his fidelity and love for us.

For years, my faith was tested as I prayed again and again for relief, but the pain persisted. But I trusted in God. I repeated my prayer constantly: *Lord, heal my back. Yet, not my will but yours be done.*

Then one day, at a charismatic conference on signs and wonders, something happened. The seminar reminded me of a college chemistry class. There was a session of teaching and then there was lab time. At the end of every session, we would wait on the Lord and ask him to move according to his will. There was no revved-up emotionalism, no music that manipulated our feelings and tugged on our heartstrings (or purse strings). This was simply a time to open our hearts to God with honesty and integrity.

During the breaks, I would go outside away from everyone and stretch my back or even lay on the grass. Those breaks, just like every moment of my life, were consumed with pain. Of course, the seminar had me thinking about healing. I had hope that I would be healed, but certainly did not expect it. I trusted fully in God's love and perfect will.

Finally, during an afternoon session, my back could not take it anymore. I found a bench out of sight in the back entryway and lay down. By the coffee break, I felt a little better, so I got up and went back into the main room. As the session ended, one of the instructors said that he had a sense that God was healing someone of a back problem.

I was hopeful that the word was for me, but on the other hand, so many people have back problems that I figured the man's claim was pretty generic. I wasn't being cynical. I just figured that out of the several hundred people in the room, most of them had some degree of back pain. If the session leader wanted to manipulate the audience, calling out back pain seemed like an easy way to do so. And if he was being sincere and God was at work, how could I assume the word was intended for me?

Then the leader said that the injury occurred while the sufferer was carrying bricks. That hit me like...well, like a ton of bricks. The second time that I had dropped to my knees racked, with back pain, I was carrying some bricks. The moment that word was spoken, my body and soul were flooded with the power of God. Any trace of cynicism or doubt was gone, and I knew God was healing me.

I raised my hand and they asked me to come forward. They prayed for me, but the pain did not go away. Still, I didn't have any doubts. I *knew* that God had healed me. While I was praying with them in a side room, someone else came in and said they felt like they had to share something. They were a little hesitant, but said, "Did you ever get injured kicking someone in a fight or something?"

I began to tremble, tears and a grin both on my face. This was really happening.

"Yes! The first time my back blew out, I was in the dojo doing roundhouse kicks to a kicking bag in karate."

We finished praying and then they looked at me, "How do you feel?"

I smiled, "I do not feel any different, but I know that God healed me. I believe God has healed the damaged part of my back, and the residual pain and inflammation will gradually go away."

Sure enough, I began to feel better and better over the coming days, until finally I was walking through the grocery store and had the sudden realization that I had no back pain. I wish I could express how great a miracle this is in my life.

My back became God's back and my weakness was infused with his strength. The words of St. Paul in 2 Corinthians 12:10 continue to echo in my heart: "I am content with weaknesses, insults, hardships, persecutions, and calamities; for whenever I am weak, then I am strong." Even now, as I lean over to type this, I remember as I do almost every moment of my life that God healed me decades ago. Almost with every breath I breathe, I remember that by God's grace and the prayer of faith, I was healed.

When I became a champion tandem surfer, I knew it was only by God's grace, and that it would be an empty award unless it opened the door to share the incredibly good news of God's power and love. I knew that day, as I know now, that that trophy belonged to God, for he used my weakness to demonstrate his glory.

For years, my back pain was a mountain I could not overcome in my life. But the faith of those who prayed with and for me at the seminar moved the mountain of my pain by God's grace. The virtue of faith that can move mountains is available to you, too. If you are a Christian, you get to do the stuff that Jesus said you would do. In Mark 16, Jesus says, "And these signs will accompany those who believe: by using my name they will cast out demons...they will lay their hands on the sick, and they will recover" (vv. 17–18).

My son Shane was on a three-month mission trip in

Katmandu. His job was behind the camera, filming. One day they walked deep into the jungle to a remote village, and he saw an elderly woman sitting in the middle of town. As they walked in, she looked up, surprised to see visitors. She reached out and Shane could see through his lens that her arm was deformed and that she had some sort of rot festering on her forearm. Shane was filled with compassion, and in faith, he set down his camera, took her arm in his hands, and prayed for her. Before his eyes, she was miraculously healed.

Jesus said that we will do even greater works than he did on earth. What could be greater than his raising the dead, calming the seas, and healing the sick? After Christ ascended into heaven, God sent the Holy Spirit to "teach you everything, and remind you of all that I have said to you" (John 14:26). Through the Holy Spirit, we can see people's souls healed from sin in Christ's name. We can witness walls of bitterness and violence torn down by grace and mercy. We have been given dominion over demons, and, at the name of Jesus, they flee. But these things pale in comparison to seeing the birth of faith in a person. By the Holy Spirit, we are able to lead people to an encounter with Christ. Seeing people grow in faith to move past their mountain of doubt to experience Christ's salvation is the greatest work of all.

If you are in God's will, you will see mountains move. This starts by setting daily times of prayer. If you start out in the morning with prayer and end your day in prayer, you will soon find that your whole day is a prayer. However you choose to pray—the rosary, the Liturgy of the Hours, or simply turning your heart to God at certain times of the day—keeping these daily appointments with God will help you intercede with greater power and confidence. When I pray the rosary, and ask Jesus's mother to take the needs I am praying about to her son, I know I have the best possible prayer partner.

The virtue of faith takes a leap into God's will, resting fully in the knowledge of his sovereignty and grace. When we are willing to leap and able to rest, our faith moves mountains. If we would walk the way of heroic virtue, we must move in faith as prayer warriors.

CHAPTER TWENTY-ONE

THE WAY OF HEROIC VIRTUE: MOTHER ANGELICA

The first time I walked down the long hallway toward the reception room of EWTN, I saw a portrait of Mother Angelica smiling at me with a mischievous look in her eye. She seemed to be saying, "It's about time you got here. Are you ready to rock the boat and have some fun?" I couldn't help it; I responded out loud, "Yes, Mother Angelica, I am ready to have some fun!"

Even though I had long been a fan of EWTN, I wondered how this whole network came to be. I knew she had started it, but I didn't know the details. Just who was Mother Angelica?

You probably guessed that the name Angelica is not Mother's birth name. The name under her picture in the high school yearbook is Rita. Rita was a drum majorette, and even though she kept to herself in school, she was the leader of the band. Her father abandoned the family when Rita was young. Feisty little Rita wasn't about to let him get away with ignoring them, though, and would hunt through the bars of Canton, Ohio, for him, demanding that he pay his support money. Those checks were few and far between, but her mother worked hard to support her family.

In her teenage years, Rita became deathly ill from a stomach ailment that required many abdominal surgeries, many of which did not seem to work. She was frail and continued to drop weight, and her situation soon became dire. She was advised to offer a nine-day prayer, or novena, with the assurance that God would cure her.

After the ninth day passed, she awoke to the sharpest stomach pain she had ever felt. As it eased, she heard a voice telling her to stand up and walk without her stomach brace. She jumped out of bed, marched into the kitchen, and told her grandmother she wanted a pork chop, insisting she had been healed. She pulled up her pajama top to show her stomach. The big lump and blue discoloration that had been there were gone.

Rita soon joined a cloistered Franciscan convent, taking the name Angelica. She felt called by God to go to Alabama and start a convent there. Once there, her teaching became so popular in the local area that she was inspired to distribute little booklets of her lessons. Soon, the demand for her booklets became so great that Mother Angelica ordered a printing press for the convent, trusting that God would provide the funds. He did.

The printing business grew rapidly. Mother Angelica and her fellow cloistered nuns were a powerhouse of work and prayer. The sign above the print shop read, "The Master's Print Shop. We don't know what we're doing, but we are getting good at it."

Eventually, twenty-five thousand books rolled off those presses every day. Soon they were duplicating cassette tapes, too. Still, this was just the beginning. After Mother visited a Christian television studio in Chicago and saw a satellite dish that could beam programs to space and then back to earth, she decided she needed to get one. Before long, the Eternal Word Television Network was born.

Mother Angelica's small steps of faith became giant leaps of faith. At every turn she rested in God's will, trusting that he was guiding each step. By faith and hard work, Mother Angelica and her sisters expanded the television network and began to develop a global radio network. With each new and more ambitious calling, Mother Angelica responded with confident assurance in God's sovereignty.

No obstacle could shake Mother Angelica's faith in God. If he wanted a nun with no knowledge of publishing to buy a printing press, then fine. If he called her to start a television network, she'd do it. If he wanted a radio antenna built on a hill that professionals say is inaccessible, she would be sure to build it there. Leap after leap. Mountain after mountain. Mother Angelica walked in the way of heroic virtue.

The noise of the surf sucks away the sound of his scream. I wait a brief moment, then return to his wife, who is holding her position anxiously.

"Is he OK?" she asks.

I look for the telltale signs of wipeout. If his surfboard, which is connected to his leg by the leash, was standing in the water like a tombstone, it meant he'd been drilled down deep and was being held under.

I smile at her, "He probably had the rush of his life, but I think he made it."

I see another wave looming up behind her and am thankful she can't see how big it is. It seemed the swell had grown by half again since I first caught up with them.

This will be sketchy, I think as I position her on her board ten feet in front of me and to my right. I tell her to scoot back about six inches so that her feet are barely trailing off the back.

"I think this will definitely be something to write home about," I joke.

"Well you only live onc—" Her words trail off when she catches sight of the wave rolling up on us. Her face pales.

"PADDLE!" I order, hoping my command will startle her into action and prevent her from freezing up.

It works. She lowers her head and starts to paddle. I feel the wave lifting me, and I begin to slide down its face toward her. I push the back of her board to help her get into the wave. To the left, I can see the water starting to bowl in on itself. This will not be a smooth entry. It will be a free-fall air drop with no parachute.

I make a lightning-fast change in plans. Instead of pushing her board forward, I scramble to grab her leash and sit way back on my own board. I pull the nose back, trying not to drop in, while at the same time pulling back hard on her leash to try to stop her from going over the falls, too. A flood of memories of bad wipeouts filled my mind. As the wave surges under us, I remember being launched into the pit of another wave, much like this one. That day, I was drilled down by the force of the wave so deeply that it pinned me to the reef. I know that this woman would not survive something like that. She is too exhausted and scared. I pull back on her leash and push my own memories aside.

The
Virtue
of
Hope

THE SEA BECKONS

Sometimes, in the middle of the night, I wake up to the sound of surf outside my open window. The sounds stirs a dream within me of a massive, beautiful wave rolling out in the deep blue ocean more than a hundred miles out to sea. I always hope that I have an appointment with that wave in the coming day. As Song of Solomon 3:1 sings, "Upon my bed by night I sought him whom my soul loves."

I get up a few hours later and pour a morning cup of Kona coffee and then, full of anticipation and excitement, I look out over the ocean to the horizon. I am always filled with hope, longing for that perfect wave. After I wax up my board, I'll paddle about a mile and a half to a reef we call Fours. This reef bends the wave into a right-hand turn as the off-shore trade winds blow, holding the wave up, sculpting and hollowing it out before it finally throws. I know that if I time my drop perfectly, and fade a little to the left before powering a bottom turn to the right, then I might find myself deep in the wave, surfing the tube hidden in the barrel of that wave.

There is a longing in all of us for that perfect wave, that perfect free-throw shot, that perfect long pass, or the perfect diffusion of light as the sunset shines through a breaking wave. There is something in humanity that is drawn to the beauty of perfection and a desire to be one with it.

Every romantic novel ever written is really only tapping into that desire deep within us to love and be loved, not just by another creature, but by our Creator. The yearning to connect with beauty, to intimately share our lives with someone, and to seek perfection comes from the very core of our being because it is actually the deep longing for intimacy with our Creator. It is a longing that he placed within us, and one he longs to fill. To pursue that longing—to seek the knowledge of God—is to have the virtue of hope.

The *Catechism* says:

> Hope is the theological virtue by which we desire the kingdom of heaven and eternal life as our happiness, placing our trust in Christ's promises and relying not on our own strength, but on the help of the grace of the Holy Spirit. Let us hold fast the confession of our hope without wavering, for he who promised is faithful. "The Holy Spirit...he has poured out upon us richly through Jesus Christ our Savior, so that we might be justified by his grace and become heirs in hope of eternal life" (Titus 3:6–7). (1817)

Every time I make the long paddle out to the lineup, my eyes scan the horizon in anticipation, hoping for a perfect wave. Six to eight miles out is where you see the lines of the bigger surf rolling along like the back of a huge whale. I love this view. I am paddling out to the surf, but in a more powerful and awesome way, that wave is coming to me. The ocean is a metaphor for God in this way. The farther into it I travel, the closer it comes to me.

If we paddle out, the wave will come to us. Nobody can surf from the shore. You must turn your sights to the sea, paddle out, and seek the wave. The Word promises us that "when you search for me, you will find me; if you seek me with all your heart, I will let you find me" (Jeremiah 29:13–14). This is the source of our hope as Christians, for it gives us confidence to face whatever the future might bring, "for surely I know the plans I have for you, says the Lord, plans for your welfare and not for harm, to give you a future with hope" (Jeremiah 29:11).

This is our hope—that as we turn to God, he will meet us here in our lives today, for God is never far. He is as close as the next breath. Like surfers, we must leave the shore and seek him, always hoping for that perfect wave. Once we've paddled out, we wait. We look to the horizon for what we long for. We hope. Once we've turned our back on the land and abandoned our will to God's, we've given up all control. We cannot make the surf build, we cannot make the waves. Even so, we wait in hope and in prayer for the presence of the Lord. We know that "whoever would approach him must believe that he exists and that he rewards those who seek him" (Hebrews 11:6).

Hope is that wellspring in us that desires happiness. The *Catechism* addresses the connection between hope and happiness:

> The virtue of hope responds to the aspiration to happiness which God has placed in the heart of every man; it takes up the hopes that inspire man's activities and purifies them so as to order them to the Kingdom of heaven. Hope keeps man from discouragement; it sustains him during times of abandonment; it opens up his heart in expectation of eternal beatitude. Buoyed up by hope, he is preserved from selfishness and led to the happiness that flows from charity. (1818)

It is OK to want to be happy. God placed that desire in us. The ancient surfer adage is to never turn your back on the ocean. Waves have been known to come and grab people right off the beach. But we do need to turn our back on the *aina*, the land. In other words, we cannot keep our focus on the temporal, but must turn our eyes to the ocean of God's eternal love.

The virtues are all interconnected. To enter the ocean of God's love takes faith as well as hope. Navigating the currents of our lives takes both prudence and self-mastery. And of course, pushing past waves of doubt or hurt takes fortitude.

We cannot embrace only one of the virtues and leave the rest behind. To know the fullness of God's wild and untamable adventure, we have to embrace each virtue, understanding that they all depend on one another.

The virtues of hope and fortitude can be very similar, and yet very different. As I said, fortitude is like a fullback who lowers his head and plows through the opposition with his own iron-willed determination. Hope, on the other hand, is like a wide receiver looking up with his arms extended, waiting for the perfect pass. As Scripture instructs us, "stand up and raise your heads, because your redemption is drawing near" (Luke 21:28). We can reach up in hope, knowing that God will not fail us, no matter the situation, since "hope does not disappoint us, because God's love has been poured into our hearts through the Holy Spirit who has been given to us" (Romans 5:5).

A young college freshman and participant on a recent Deep Adventure Retreat nailed it when he said, "Hope is the first step of faith." Hope is not a passive thing. God wants our hope to cause us to lean into the wind and pull one more paddle stroke against the tide, against the rip, against the ocean current. He wants us to have faith in his promises, and to trust that he has plans for our welfare. This trust should fuel our hope, driving us farther into the ocean of his love, for we know that he will meet us in those rolling waters.

The best way to keep our hope alive and active is to have daily times of prayer and meditation on his Word and practice faithful reception of the sacraments. Turn your face to the sea by praying the Liturgy of the Hours, meditating on the Word, or praying the rosary. Many people find a deep encounter with God as they sit in the presence of Jesus's body, blood, soul, and divinity—all present in the Eucharist. It is through these acts—prayer, reading the Scriptures, and the sacraments—that our hope is renewed.

When you are in prayer, you sometimes don't sense that anything is happening within your nature. Sometimes we focus on the waiting and don't recognize what is already being done. A surfer is not conscious of the fact that, as he waits for a wave, his hair is being bleached by the sun and salt, and his skin is growing more bronze. He hopes for the wave, but the simple act of waiting is changing him.

I remember sitting on my surfboard on a beautiful calm day, barely a wave in the water. There was very little hope of catching a wave. But still, I waited as the sun sank toward the horizon. Suddenly, out of the depth, a gray whale surfaced just a few feet from me. The magnificent creature hung out for a minute, watching me watch him, before disappearing into the blue. As we wait and hope on the Lord, he is already changing us. We have no idea what great things God is doing below the surface, but we know he is working. We may not see it now, but some day it will be revealed. So let us wait with him in hope.

CHAPTER TWENTY-THREE

EAGLE'S REST

My sister Tammy walked out of the hospital room in frustration, saying, "Someday I will ask God." I looked up, "Ask him what?"

"Why our mom—this incredible, courageous, woman who just emanates God's joy and love—has suffered so much in her life."

Tammy wasn't exaggerating in either aspect. Our mom was incredible and courageous and had taught me so much about God as a living example. But her life had also been fraught with suffering.

My mother's father left her family when she was a small child, and her mother died in childbirth soon after. My mom was tossed around from one relative's home to another, and separated most of the time from her brother and two sisters.

The only consolation that she found whenever she was lonely was when she would sit after school in the local parish in her little town of Leola, South Dakota. It was the only place she felt true peace. She later came to realize that it was the presence of Jesus in the Eucharist that was bringing her this peace. At the age of fourteen, she became a Catholic. Sadly, this resulted in her being kicked out of the house where she had been staying. She was on her own.

Eventually, she moved to California to join her sister in the Bay Area, where she met my dad. My mother and father went on a couple of dates, but my dad had to go back to North Dakota to finish college. My mom felt that she needed to catch her breath and discern God's direction for her life. An opportunity arose to stay in a convent where she could seek solitude and protection from the world, and she took it. She did not correspond with anyone except for my dad. When he showed up unexpectedly to greet her in the abbey garden, any question she might have had about her future vanished.

Twenty years and four children later, she fell into a deep, hormone-related depression and didn't leave her room for more than a year. An incredible doctor worked with her to restore her hormonal balance, and in time, we got our mom back. Five years later, she began to suffer from a degenerative arterial disease. Over the course of a few decades, she had thirteen life-threatening and painful surgeries, one of which resulted in a stroke that greatly impaired her speaking ability for the rest of her life. She understood everything we said, but when she wanted to say something the wrong words came out. Despite all that, her constant joy and smile communicated everything.

A few months before my sister's frustrated outburst, my mom needed to have a good portion of her leg amputated due to lack of blood flow and extreme pain. The circulation to the surgical site remained so weak that the wound never healed. An ensuing infection proved incurable. The doctor's news confirmed our deep fear: We were going to lose her.

My mother suffered more than anyone I have ever known and yet, though she would cry out when she had a sudden burst of pain, she remained valiant and never once complained. I have never known anyone with a greater hope, love, or joy. Though she could not speak very well, her joyful acceptance and smile spoke homilies.

One morning in March 2013, I walked into her hospital room as dawn was breaking and opened the curtains. It was winter, and her room overlooked the Mississippi River in St. Cloud, Minnesota. The gorgeous, cloudy, snow-swept landscape made me forget for an instant why I was there. The beauty and sorrow of that moment made me want to nestle deeper into the warmth of the family that surrounded me.

Just below Mom's window, the mighty Mississippi flowed under the ice. Just like God's constant love, it flowed, unseen and unheard. Just like God's humble power, the river surged below the surface of the ice with relentless strength, sweeping away anything in its path. And again, just as God lets himself be contained by the banks of our frail being, the river stayed within the banks formed by the earth. That beautiful, snowy day, my sleepy family gathered close in my mom's hospital room. We all sensed it was a sacred place. She was in a coma and had received the anointing of the sick just a few days before, which had helped give my father peace about her imminent passing. My father was sleeping restfully on a cot next to her bed, as he had done for days. The fragrant, half-dozen plumeria and tuberose Hawaiian leis I had brought from home were draped across her blanket.

As Dad slept, the rhythm of his breath matched hers. As a deacon in the Catholic Church, he had spoken all over the world, but he insisted that it was my mother who was the wind beneath my wings. I thought of their North Shore home, Eagle's Rest, and the big welcome sign with a familiar verse etched beneath: "Those who wait for the LORD shall renew their strength, they shall mount up with wings like eagles" (Isaiah 40:31).

At that moment in the hospital, it was as if my parents were two eagles flying in silent formation toward her new home. My father has spent many, many nights of his life sleeping in uncomfortable chairs and cots in hospital rooms, tenderly caring for my mother's needs. When my father woke up, he leaned forward and whispered to her, "Mereece, it's OK. You can go home now. I love you, my beautiful bride. You can go home now."

As he spoke, something incredible happened. A bald eagle soared within ten feet of the hospital window. We all turned to watch its flight in amazement. It returned for another pass and then did one long loop right next to the window again before soaring away. We watched it until it flew out of view. Then we became aware of an obvious shallowing in my mother's labored breathing as she began to glow with a beautiful radiance. Even her skin seemed to become youthful.

Within a few moments of the eagle's flight, my mother took flight, too. She had been in a coma for a week, and yet, with her final three breaths, she said with a strong, astonishing, and joyful voice, "Oh! Oh! Oh!" We had no doubt that she was seeing the beatific vision. As the clock shone 8:11 a.m. on the same date as their marriage sixty-two years earlier, the twin virtues of hope and faith carried her on wings like eagles to heaven. Now in heaven, they are enfolded, for there is no need for faith or hope in heaven. For all we have had faith in and hoped for, we now clearly see; and all that remains is love.

My mother knew joy not because her life was perfect, but because she suffered. Suffering is our great gift on the path to transformation. Like a caterpillar in the cocoon that emerges as a butterfly, we too are transformed in the embrace of suffering. Do not reject the dark night of the soul. To walk the way of the hero, we must learn to find joy in our suffering as we cooperate with God's grace on our journey toward intimacy with him.

St. John of the Cross taught that suffering is the sweetest of sorrows. The dark night of the soul teaches us to love God, not out of fear of hell or because of what he does for us, but because of whom God is. In the dark night, we understand that we are beggars with a poverty of spirit, yet he sustains and infuses us with love and life. In our weakness, he is strong. Through suffering, we—like the saints—learn to walk ever closer to our Lord.

Saints fully surrender themselves to God while on this earth. A saint is someone who joyfully endures suffering for the sake of purgation on their way to nuptial love with God here on earth, so that they need not go through purgatory after death. How many saints lived in poverty, faced disease and persecution, or died as martyrs? Both suffering and joy are part of the life of every saint, just as it was part of Jesus's life.

What is true of the lives of the saints, is true for us as well. By responding in trust to the love of God in suffering, great joy is born—joy so deep and rich that nothing on this earth can steal it away. Like David, those who suffer can sing praises to God because "you have turned my mourning into dancing; / you have taken off my sackcloth / and clothed me with joy" (Psalm 30:11).

Do you feel that you are in a dark place right now and you can't seem to sense God? Instead of thinking you are alone, consider that you might merely be wrapped in the cocooning arms of Christ's suffering. Don't lose heart. Though you may feel that the light of his love for you has gone out, in reality, his light is shining so brightly that you are blinded.

I remember doing a nighttime tandem surfing exhibition in Biarritz, France, with twenty thousand people watching from the cliffs of Cote de Basque. As we turned to paddle for the wave, I was blinded by the stadium lights above and spotlights below that shone toward the water so that the crowd could see us. I had to put my partner into a lift by sensing the wave instead of seeing it. So it is when we feel alone in our suffering. Though you feel that you are in darkness, in fact, his blinding light is illuminating you. You can choose either to abandon your faith in the darkness or to rely on your faith, moving forward in the hope that the wave of his ever-present love will carry you, even when you cannot see him.

My mother suffered in nearly every possible way that a person can suffer. Tammy's frustrated question was answered in that moment when our mom glowed and spoke aloud as she went to her Beloved. Her suffering led her on a journey of total yielding of her life to God while on earth. Though she was rarely released from the cocoon of suffering on earth, she chose hope. She chose happiness and joy. She walked the way of heroic virtue.

CHAPTER TWENTY-FOUR

THE WAY OF THE HEROIC VIRTUE: ST. DAMIEN AND ST. MARIANNE

The cliffs of Kalaupapa, Hawaii, are more than two thousand feet high in places, dropping down into deep blue water. These picturesque cliffs provide a panoramic view of the horizon, and in 1873, they welcomed St. Damien of Molokai into the dark history of the island. At that time, Molokai was home to hundreds of exiles who were imprisoned by those sea cliffs and the ocean as they suffered the agonies of leprosy.

Leprosy, now known as Hansen's disease, causes damage to nerve cells and can prevent the sufferer from feeling pain, resulting in repeated injury, infection, and the inability to heal. The extreme disfigurement and infection that can occur with the disease made it seem as if those suffering from leprosy were rotting alive, and prompted societies to force lepers out of the community. Molokai hosted Hawaii's leper colony, and its remoteness was so isolating that few healthy individuals dared to provide care for those forced to live there.

The colony could only be reached by boat, and the passage through the channel between Molokai and O'ahu to the Kalaupapa Peninsula was treacherous. If the winds were blowing hard, which happened often, the boats couldn't reach shore, and the ill passengers were forced to jump into the water and swim. Many exiles died before they even made it to Kalaupapa.

When St. Damien first arrived to Kalaupapa as a vigorous young man, he found that he would be ministering to as many as fifteen hundred exiles. There were only a few ramshackle buildings, no church, and no real medical care. There was also no escape from the area, surrounded as it was by sea and towering cliffs. St. Damien immediately set to work, digging out a narrow path with more than twenty-four switchbacks that led up the vertical slope, past the mountain goats, to the rest of the island. At times he would hike to the top of the mountain and find *paniolos* (cowboys) to round up some cattle and drive them right off the edge of the *pali* (cliff) so that the desperate exiles below would have food.

Though his efforts to ease the suffering of those in the colony were great, it still broke his heart that he was unable to touch, bathe, or comfort them. Little was known about the disease at the time, and it wasn't uncommon for caretakers to become infected if they came into physical contact with a sufferer. Finally, compassion moved St. Damien to disregard his own safety and to live with the lepers as equals, providing them the simple comfort and hope of physical touch as he cared for them. He even dipped his fingers into the same bowl of *poi* as everyone else.

After sixteen years of living with and caring for those in the colony, St. Damien contracted the disease as well. As his health failed, another came to offer hope to the exiles. St. Marianne Cope arrived, ready to continue St. Damien's work. One of the first things he showed her was the top joint of his thumb and the index finger of the hand with which he raised the consecrated Host during Mass. There was no sign of leprosy there.

St. Marianne had grown up working hard to care for those she loved. Her father was an invalid, and as a child, she worked in a textile factory to help support the family. When her father passed away, she pursued her vocation as a nun. In 1883, a call was sent out to over fifty religious congregations for help in Molokai. St. Marianne responded eagerly.

She said, "I am hungry for the work and I wish with all my heart to be one of the chosen Ones, whose privilege it will be, to sacrifice themselves for the salvation of the souls of the poor Islanders.... I am not afraid of any disease, hence, it would be my greatest delight even to minister to the abandoned 'lepers.'"[14]

In notes from a sermon that he preached in 1883, St. Damien observed that those who are lepers now, will no longer be lepers in heaven. Though he could not promise them a cure, the priest could bring to them the hope of Christ by identifying with them in their suffering. Even before he contracted the disease, St. Damien stood in solidarity when he spoke of "We Lepers."[15] He began more and more to speak to them as exiles and not lepers, for he saw us all as exiles on this earth.

Under his guidance, the colony was transformed. Basic laws were established, housing improved, schools built, and farming organized. When St. Damien died in April of 1889, the whole community followed his funeral procession to his final resting place.

Some say it is a miracle that St. Marianne never contracted the disease as she ministered hope to the exiles. Her work, like St. Damien's, was tireless. She set up the Malulani Hospital in Maui, combatted another hospital's administrative abuse of leprosy patients, and was given full oversight of the Branch Hospital at Kakaako near Honolulu. She was canonized by Pope Benedict XVI on October 21, 2012.

The saints of Molokai brought hope to the hopeless on Molokai. When the beatification of St. Damien was under consideration and the Vatican sought evidence of a miracle being done through his intercession, Mother Teresa sent a letter to Pope John Paul II saying, "I know a miracle. The birth of hope is a miracle."[16]

I pulled myself back over the edge of the wave, losing sight of her as she disappeared on the other side. I hoped the leash would hold. After a moment, I saw the tail of her board come flying through the lip of the wave, the rest of it following as she clung to it, too frightened to scream.

She was about to drop into a terrible wipeout. I yanked on the leash, hauling her away from the edge just before she dropped into the wave. Her face was pale with shock when she turned toward me again, and I couldn't help but grin.

"I didn't think you would like that one," I said.

She barked a small, relieved laugh, "Ya think?"

Another wave was headed our way, this one with more south to it. This was our shot.

"Here we go...we want this one. Get ready. OK, PADDLE!"

She responded immediately, paddling with all her might along with me. When her board dropped over the precipice, mine followed and I caught up with her and pushed hers slightly to the right.

"HOLD ON!" I shouted as her surfboard careened down the face of the wave. She gripped the edges with white knuckles, riding the wave like it was a bucking bronco and screaming as she went. I stood, surfing along behind her, keeping an eye out for her husband or his surfboard. They were nowhere to be seen.

Every ten yards she traveled decreased the chances of an avalanche of water dumping on top of her. Her scream never faded as I rode about twenty feet to the left of her. I reached my hand into the face of the wave to slow me down a bit. It was a beautiful wave, and I was tempted to stall right there and tuck into the barrel of water that was gaping open just a few feet behind me. I resisted, knowing she might end up in jeopardy if the wave shot me out like a cannon. We fired down the line toward a dozen surfers who were hanging out, hooting for her as she blew by.

The ride lasted no more than thirty seconds, but for her, it must have felt like an eternity. The waved dumped her into a deep area of the reef in front of us before backing off. She looked at me, her face exultant for an instant. The look faded, shifting quickly into fear as she realized we were alone in the deep water. As I paddled up next to her, she twisted on her board, craning her neck to look behind her.

When she spoke, her voice was tight with anxiety, "Did you see my husband? Where is he?"

The
Virtue
of
Love

CHAPTER TWENTY-FIVE

THE KNOCK AT THE DOOR

The modern world turns on varying ideals of love, from the effusive passion of a romance novel to the exalted sensibilities of a modern hippie for all living beings. At all times and places, love is brandished, redefined, abused, and altered to reflect our personal tastes or preferences. Love has become a slogan, a hashtag, a motto. Society is quick to shout, "Love is free!" "Love wins!" "Make love, not war!" Yet these slick sayings barely scratch the surface of love, and they fail to admit or accept the foundational and absolute truth:

God is Love.

How am I to write a chapter about the virtue of love? One might as well ask, "How can one comprehend God?"

For God is impenetrable, immutable, infinite, eternal, essential essence, self-subsistent, fathomless wisdom, abiding beyond the realm of light and dark. He is pure, perfect, holy, good, omnipotent, omniscient, omnipresent, and immaterial. In him, there is no contingency, for true goodness is concomitant with his essence. All creation is dependent and contingent upon him. He is indivisible; invisible, but made visible through his handiwork; three in one, immovable, uncreated, without beginning or end, immortal, just, enlightening, immeasurable, unlimited.

Oh, and just one more thing.

God is love.

Love begins with God, exists in God, and *is* God. There is no love apart from God. All of us—whether we believe in God or not—love because God loves us, because God created humankind in his image and imbued us with his essence, his love. God loved humankind and, in particular, he loved *you* so much that he created you and gave you the greatest possible gift: himself, the gift of his love. The Bible tells us, "For God so loved the world that he gave his only Son, so that everyone who believes in him may not perish but have eternal life" (John 3:16).

St. Thomas Aquinas said that "love is willing the true good of the other."[17] God, in his infinite love for us, wills our good by offering us eternal life. Jesus said that "no one has greater love than this, to lay down one's life for one's friends" (John 15:13). And Jesus did exactly that, laying his life down for us on the cross, even "while we were enemies" and unbelieving of his love (Romans 5:10).

Our culture implies that love is all about feelings. What we feel matters, and when we no longer feel a certain way, we must be true to ourselves and do what we need to do. Or so our culture believes. In reality, feelings are the caboose on the love train. They are merely a part of love, a part that comes long after the reality of love is already present. Feelings alone have no power to fuel our love. What fuels love is the will for another's good and the act of self-donation.

That makes it so clear, doesn't it? Jesus said, "Love your enemies and pray for those who persecute you" (Matthew 5:44). See, there it is. Love isn't about feelings. Who has warm and fuzzy feelings for an enemy? No, love is about action. It's the committed desire for the good of another and enacting it. Love is a choice, and it is self-donation. Jesus commands us to make the choice of love, even for those who don't deserve it in our opinions. But Jesus leads us by exemplifying the very love he challenges us to demonstrate. Jesus gave his flesh, heart, soul, and divinity. The Father gave his Son for us. Mary gave her child. God wills good for us and demonstrated self-donation through the cross.

Love, by its very nature, creates and gives. It is because God is love that he eternally begat his son. It is because God is love that he created you. It is because God is love that he draws you into communion. As Jesus opened his arms wide on the cross, so he opens wide the door of his heart to you.

The Latin word for *love* is *caritas*. This is most closely translated as "charity." Charity is more than benevolence. It is more than giving from our excess. Charity is self-donation with no expectation of personal benefit. It is a love that seeks to give.

God is always moving in love. Let me say it more specifically: God, at all times, is moving *toward* you in active love. On earth, you cannot run away from his love, as the psalmist says, "Where can I go from your spirit? Or where can I flee from your presence?" (Psalm 139:7). Adam and Eve tried to hide, but God pursued them in the garden. His love pursues us to draw us to him. When we try to hide with our affections, agendas, attachments, distractions, and disordered desires from God, he still seeks us. He still loves us.

His love seeks us, and it is his love in us that seeks God. There is a big question within each of our souls, a question that cannot be answered by anything on earth. A question is, at its core, a *quest*. It is a seeking. We are on a quest for truth. We all quest for the meaning of life. Like God in the garden, we are seeking the one we love.

We are seeking truth. Truth is not an abstract idea. Our world considers truth a personal preference, but truth is absolute. Truth is a person and his name is Jesus. Jesus said, "I am the way, and the truth, and the life" (John 14:6). God is love, God is truth. Only in him can we find an answer to our question. Only in him do we find rest in our quest.

We do not quest alone. God, too, is on a quest. A quest for us. He is knocking on the door of your heart, seeking you.

The Word of God says, "Listen! I am standing at the door and knocking; if you hear my voice and open the door, I will come in to you and eat with you, and you with me" (Revelation 3:20). He is moving toward you in love, his arms open on the cross in invitation. It is up to you to open the door of your heart.

Hebrews 4:7 pleads, "Today, if you hear his voice, do not harden your hearts." God is knocking. Your time is limited—you must open the door. As 2 Corinthians 6:2 says, "See, now is the acceptable time; see, now is the day of salvation." Not later today, not tomorrow, the time is *now.* Stop seeking the answer to the question of your heart in what is temporary. Turn your eyes to the mark and open the door to him. Surrender all to Jesus. Invite him to live in your heart as the King and Savior. Ask forgiveness for your sins; ask for help in your unbelief and healing for your wounded nature. If you desire a personal encounter with God and ongoing conversion of heart, then ask him to make himself known to you in the deepest part of your heart. Ask, and you shall receive. Seek, and you shall find.

CHAPTER TWENTY-SIX

WRESTLING WITH GOD

Can you imagine being startled out of sleep in the middle of the deep darkness of a desert night in a full on grappling match with God? In the Old Testament we see the story of Jacob awaking to find himself in that very situation. He woke in the middle of the night—and the middle of the desert—and found he was not alone. Genesis 32:24 tells us that he "wrestled with him until daybreak." As jujitsu fighters refer to it, he was "rolling" on the desert dirt and being slammed up against car-size rocks. This was the longest mixed martial arts fight in history, with no timeouts and no referee to stop the fight.

Jacob must have been in great shape, because he fought with God all night long and even overcame his pain to cling to his opponent. Jacob refused to let go, demanding to receive a blessing. This is what fighters do when they are overmatched and cannot win or run. They close the distance and hang on for dear life so that their opponent cannot get in the full power of a punch or kick.

There comes a time in our journey toward intimacy with God that he begins to wrestle with us, too. Some cling to their earthly attachments, others to relationships that may be unhealthy. Still others cling to their own agendas and plans. In the dark night, Jesus challenges us to a battle for our very souls. It is almost like a linebacker tackling a running back while at the same time punching at the football to make him let go of it. It is up to us to choose whether we will eventually cling to God and seek his blessing, or succumb to the finite desires for which we initially wrestle.

God is love, and because he loves us, he is willing to challenge us so that our character can be strengthened by trial. He certainly allowed Jesus the dignity of free will in the desert. There, hungry and weak, Jesus faced his own wrestling match—with Satan. Satan tried to defeat Jesus with the jab of riches, the right hook of self-glory, and the uppercut of power. He taunted Jesus with the lust of the eye, the lust of the flesh, and the pride of life. Jesus countered every blow because he clung only to his Father for the sake of his Father.

If we desire true intimacy with God, we can expect times when God will drive us into the dark night and will wrestle with us as we try to cling to the world, the flesh, and the devil. He looks at us in the eyes of our heart and says, "Let go." Our arms grow tired and we can no longer grab onto our wants and desires. Like a boxer in a fight who is up against the ropes, we finally wrap our arms around our opponent, except our opponent is actually our loving God. We cling close so the blows cannot hurt us as much. When the bell sounds, Jesus raises our arms with his high over our head in testimony, making us winners by his grace.

We are in a fight to the death, and we must choose to die to the passions and disordered desires of our old fallen nature. We must learn, like St. Paul, that "I have been crucified with Christ; and it is no longer I who live, but it is Christ who lives in me" (Galatians 2:20). It is because God loves us that he fights for us to die to our own will and cling to his, for only in his will is eternal life. In order to cling to God, we have to let go of everyone and everything else. Jesus bluntly tells it like it is: "Whoever comes to me and does not hate father and mother, wife and children, brothers and sisters, yes, and even life itself, cannot be my disciple" (Luke 14:26). Jesus gave his all for us so that we would and could give our all to him. The *Catechism* says it this way: "Charity is the theological virtue by which we love God above all things for his own sake, and our neighbor as ourselves for the love of God" (1822).

God honored Jacob's refusal to let go of him, and blessed him in two ways. First, he blessed him with a new name: Israel. Receiving a new name is an act of love and reminiscent of a marital union. The lover takes on the new name received from her beloved. Revelation 2:17 tells us that Christ will give each of us "a white stone, and on the white stone is written a new name that no one knows except the one who receives it." We are not to be his servants, nor even just his friend. We are to be called to full communion as the bride of Christ.

God also blessed him by wounding him in the hip. From that day on Israel walked with a bit of hesitation to his gait. The wound he received became an everlasting reminder of just how close God was. It reminded him—as our own wounds remind us—to check in with God as we walk through our life.

Our encounter with God changes the way we walk through life. By living in the virtue of love, we see through God's eyes. As the *Catechism* says, we learn to love God and others "for the love of God" (1822). When we see a person in need, our soul hesitates and prompts us to take action. We pray for others; we give them food, shelter, or comfort. We cling close to God. Close enough to hear his heartbeat.

Living in love is active and vibrant. In fact, love is such a dynamic concept that a single word alone cannot contain its meaning. The Greek language has multiple words for love, two of which are *eros* and *agape*. Agape is the unconditional love that God has for us like parents have for their children, a love that descends from heaven. Agape is always seeking to do good for another. It is a love that descends from heaven. Eros is the desire for beauty and perfection and the word is also used for sexual passion. Eros inspires us to pursue that deep longing in our souls and to transcend the corporeal world.

The same Jacob who wrestled with God also had a dream of a ladder that ascended to heaven, on which angels were climbing up and down between heaven and earth. I picture it as one of those ladders with two sets of legs that is hinged at the top. As I previously pointed out, the Latin root word for the cardinal virtues is *cardes,* which means "hinge." Our spiritual lives hinge on the virtues, like the top of one of these ladders.

As we climb up one side of the ladder, we grow in the cardinal virtues of justice, prudence, temperance, and fortitude. As we ascend, we see God more and more clearly, and we gradually learn to cherish him, not for what he does for us, but simply for who he is. The other set of rungs, those descending back to earth, are the theological virtues of faith, hope, and love.

Jacob's dream helps us understand agape and eros love. We ascend toward God in eros, which is a love that desires to possess. This is eros for God. We want to possess the perfect communion with God. But we climb the ladder carrying a backpack full of the things to which we cling. The spiritual longing for truth propels us to the top of the ladder. At the top of the ladder, we wrestle with God, and must choose to let go of all our attachments that are not of God. Once we have let go, we are ready to descend again, infused with agape for him. God blesses us, like he did Jacob, and we are able to live a love of self-donation for God's sake. As Luke 17:33 promises, "Those who try to make their life secure will lose it, but those who lose their life will keep it."

St. Augustine shows us this progression from eros to union with God in agape when he said, "Yet I love a certain kind of light, and sound, and fragrance, and food, and embracement in loving my God,…where that light shine unto my soul which no place can contain, where that sounds which time snatches not away, where there is fragrance which no breeze disperses."[18]

The *Catechism* tells us that the virtue of love (or charity) is "the virtue by which we love God above all things for his own sake, and our neighbor as ourselves for the love of God" (1822). It is agape, which enables us to live in this virtue. We descend the ladder, rung by rung, first by loving God for his own sake, then by loving others, and then by loving ourselves for the love of God. It is eros that gives us the desire to "taste and see that the Lord is good" (Psalm 34:8). Even a small taste of God makes our longing for him grow. As we continue in grace even through dark nights of wrestling, he faithfully leads us to abandon ourselves that we might be filled with agape for him. As my friend Girard Middleton said at one of our Deep Adventure Quests, "In the end, love is the only thing that makes sense."

THE VIRTUE OF LOVE

CHAPTER TWENTY-SEVEN
THE WAY OF HEROIC VIRTUE: EDDIE AND CLYDE AIKAU

At a young age, Eddie Aikau had earned so much respect as a big wave rider that he had been stationed as the first north shore lifeguard at the most famous big wave spot in the world, Waimea Bay. Soon after, his brother, Clyde, joined him. For ten years, the Aikau brothers never lost a single person, despite Waimea Bay's reputation for having a high death toll. They performed incredible heroic rescues using just a pair of fins and a surfboard.

Eddie was ranked in the top twelve on the International Surfing Tour and in 1978 even won the most prestigious event in the world, the Duke Kahanamoku Classic. But Eddie was more than a respected waterman. In spite of his youth, his waterman skills put him in the unique position of building bridges between visiting surfers and the local *hui*. In the surfing world, it's often said that local Hawaiians are territorial in the water and to some extent this is true. But Hawaiians have a special legacy in the water. Surfing is a rite of passage, and the relationship Hawaiian surfers have with the ocean is no different than the familiarity and sense of ownership you have with your own house. When outsiders—no matter how skillful—paddle out at some spots in Hawaii, it is no different than a stranger walking into your family room, kicking back on the couch, and watching your TV. It may sound extreme to those who don't understand the culture, but to Hawaiians, the ocean is their home even more than the land.

When a group of young, brash Australians first came to compete in the early pro events in Hawaii, they did not make an effort to understand or follow local customs, greatly offending the Hawaiian surf community. The brashness and boisterous manner of a couple of them was so contrary to the quiet strength so valued in Hawaiian culture and so alienating to the local surfers, that the Aussies soon feared for their lives. It was like a huge cleanup set about to explode on a shallow reef.

One evening, there was a knock on the front door of the house where the Australian surfers were laying low. To their relief, it was Eddie standing at the door. Even the Aussies respected Eddie, so when he told them to come with him for their own safety, they didn't hesitate. He took them to the Turtle Bay Hilton. The Aussies noticed that the parking lot of the hotel was jammed with pickups, vans, and other local cars, each adorned with surfboard racks and bumper stickers. They couldn't help but wonder what was going on.

Eddie led them into a meeting room with his brother Clyde standing by. More than one hundred Hawaiian surfers were gathered inside, and the moment they spotted the Australian surfers, they began hurling angry words at them. For a moment, it seemed the mob would rush them, but Eddie stood up, his calm strength silencing the room. He asked for one Hawaiian at a time to speak his or her piece as the Aussies sat quietly, listening to each testament.

One by one the Hawaiians began the process of making things *pono* (good). Each person explained the roots of surfing and the Hawaiian way of *aloha*, some gently and some in anger. That night the outsiders experienced an important Hawaiian tradition of communication and reconciliation, a session that went on for nearly two hours. Finally the Aussies were given their turn to speak, and they profusely apologized for their actions and attitude. Because they had sought forgiveness, the men were welcomed into the community and were able to return to the ocean. Eddie's deep love for the entire surfing community had propelled him to be a peacemaker that day and is still bearing fruit decades later. Although the initial reconciliation took place over thirty years ago, I recently surfed with one of these Aussies. When we paddled in, he was warmly greeted with respect and aloha by the locals.

Eddie's love was not limited to the surfing *ohana* (family). He loved all of the people of Hawaii and their heritage. As a result, he was an obvious choice to be a part of the initial crew of the double-hulled sailing canoe, Hokulea. The crew set sail on a two-thousand-five-hundred-mile voyage to retrace the path of the ancient Polynesians who had first discovered the Hawaiian Islands. The exemplary navigational skills and uncompromising grit of the ancient Polynesians is the pride of the Hawaiian heritage, and Eddie and his crew wanted to honor their legacy with their own commemorative voyage.

The iconic Hokulea sailed without a compass, without radio communication, and without any other modern means to find Tahiti. The first forty miles of the sail were the most treacherous because they had to cross the channel between O'ahu and Molokai. As darkness fell, gale force winds began to whip up the waves all around them. The hulls of the canoe started to take on water. Suddenly, a rogue wave hit them and they capsized. As the crew clung to the hull, Eddie knew someone had to go for help. The decision was easy: Eddie would go. And so he did.

He grabbed his rescue board and pushed off toward the island of Lanai, which was more than five miles away. His crew watched him paddle into the darkness, on his way to find help. Eddie disappeared beyond the rising swell, never to be seen again.

The next day the rest of the crew was rescued but Eddie was never found. A pilot said he had glimpsed Eddie's board in the water, but there was no one on it. Everyone in the boat knew that Eddie had made the ultimate sacrifice of love. He laid down his life for his friends.

Eddie's brother Clyde never forgot his brother's sacrifice and continues to live a life that demonstrates love and service. He does incredible work to ensure that homeless children get education and are cared for. He had a significant impact on my three sons Jeremiah, Shane, and Josh when they were younger as they each in turn worked for years next to him on the beach. Clyde became an uncle and an example to them, challenging them daily to work hard and to live aloha in the Aikau tradition.

Now, the most prestigious big wave contest in the world is held in Eddie's honor. It is called, appropriately, the Eddie, and the best surfing talent from around the globe comes by invitation only. There is a three-month holding period as the contest organizers wait for waves with at least thirty-foot faces. Clyde won the first Eddie, paddling far into the ocean and waiting for the perfect wave. His win was a heartbreaking and beautiful tribute to his brother.

The next time the event was held, the surf was so big and breaking in a pattern that made the surf out of control and impossible to ride. Each day the contest director came down before sunrise to see if he could call for the Eddie to be held, but the conditions remained too treacherous. After several days, the waves were huge but they had cleaned up bit.

The director polled the twenty-eight invitees, "Should we go?"

They were silent for a moment, looking out at the ocean. Then, one of them said quietly but firmly, "Eddie would go."

Since that day, the rallying cry for surfers around the world is, "Eddie would go!" It is a reminder that, even in the face of terrifying conditions, heroism is possible. Eddie's heroic virtue exemplified aloha. Aloha means to "give breath," and

Eddie did. He gave breath to the choked relationship between the Hawaiian and foreign surfers, establishing years of trust and friendship. He gave breath to countless people whom he resuscitated on the beach after a rescue. He even gave his last breath for the people of Hawaii when he embarked on that fateful voyage to honor their legacy. Eddie gave breath.

Eddie walked the way of the hero in the virtue of love.

In a world that desperately needs breath, needs love poured into it, Eddie would go.

Will you?

We finally see her husband about a hundred yards closer to shore. He has his back to the ocean with his face on the board. Though I'd told him to hold his position, he is paddling on, barely lifting one hand at a time. Clearly he thinks he is headed toward shore, but actually, he is making his way directly toward the next hazardous reef.

"There he is!" I point. "He looks no worse for the wear."

She laughs with relief. "We made it! We made it, we made it! That was the wildest thing I have ever done. I can't believe I'm alive."

I paddle by her so she can catch my leash. We are still an eighth of a mile from the beach but we have made it through the impact zone. There is another shallow reef ahead, but if we are careful, we can get around it.

First, I need to catch up with her husband before he paddles himself into the hazard of that reef. When we do catch up with him, he seems not to be aware of our presence. He has the thousand-yard stare of utter exhaustion. She leans over to hug him and almost falls off her board.

"Babe, we made it!"

His eyes clear as he focuses on her, and relief floods his face.

Behind them, another swell is coming on fast. We are too close to the razor-sharp reef.

"Grab her leash again. Let's roll," I say.

This time, he responds without question, holding on with both hands as he lays his head on the board. I paddle them sideways toward the beach, traveling several hundred yards to get around the reef.

The next set is almost on us. I call back to them, "Paddle off to the right of me so that we are not on top of each other. Then paddle with one hand while holding to the leash with the other. Try to catch that wave!"

I pull them into the wave and feel the tug on my leash release as they are caught up in it. A moment later, the wave backs off in deeper water. Still one-hundred-fifty yards from shore, I feel the pull on my leash subside. I look back. Without a word, the man has let go and is paddling at an angle to come into the beach a hundred yards or so away from us. He never once looks back at me.

I pull her to the shoreline and we both step off our boards into the sand. She rushes to me, giving me the biggest hug.

"You're my hero. You really saved our lives! What can we do for you?" She can't resist hugging me again.

I appreciate her gratitude, but it is starting to get embarrassing.

"Thank you. Thank you. Thank you," she gushes. She suddenly realizes her husband's absence and looks around, "Where is he?"

I point down the beach. He is just making it to shore.

"You better go get him. You guys have a good vacation."

She gives me one more hug and undoes her leash. I pull her board up on the shore as she runs toward him. He never turns or lifts a hand in thanks, even as she approaches him, calling his name with relief.

The man's response isn't unusual. I've rescued many people, and the reaction of this couple is a perfect example of the two different types of responses I've seen. For some, gratitude is shown enthusiastically and without shame. Others, though, choose to pretend the rescue never happened. The truth is, for some people, no matter how dire their situation, it is impossible to admit that they need help.

I can't help but think that Jesus knows exactly how this feels. After all, he rescued us on the cross. We were drowning in our sin, and he pulled us from the water. Some of us are grateful, but many of us still can't acknowledge we need his help. Still, Christ gives us the gift of salvation. How we react to it is our choice. I turn my board to the water. Now that they are safe, I'm eager to get back to my play. The waves are big and clean, inviting me out for some fun. The sun is warm on my back. I close my eyes for a moment and breathe in the salty air. It is a day like any other for me, and I am grateful for it. With a thrill of childlike exhilaration, I turn my back on the land and paddle out into wild and untamable ocean.

THE ROCK OF SALVATION

As St. Paul walked along his gospel road on an ancient path in Greece, he could not help but notice the stones that had been set up here and there along the way. They were referred to as *soteria* stones. Paul uses this word frequently in his writings. It is translated as "salvation." It was the practice in those days for people to set up these stones as prayers to their various gods. A woman wanting a child, an athlete on his way to compete in the Olympic Games, or a warrior going to battle may set up a stone and plead with their god for a special salvation. But these stones could not save them. St. Paul knew that the way of salvation was indeed the one rock of Jesus Christ.

When Jacob was dreaming of the ladder to heaven, his head rested on a stone as a pillow. Upon waking from the astounding dream, he poured oil over the stone to signify that God was in that place. So, too, we are called to rest on our rock of salvation. We do so by pouring out our lives like oil on a quest for deep virtue. Jesus is our *soteria* stone. He is our rock of salvation. As we walk along that ancient path, Christ himself takes our heart of stone from our bodies and gives us a heart of flesh, a heart that beats with new and right desires—*his* desires.

We see the *soteria* stones set up by those who went before us to guide us on this ancient path. The four stones of the cardinal virtues of justice, prudence, temperance, and fortitude lead us to the foot of God's mountain. Here we see the path that winds ever upward into the heavens. This path is marked by the stones of faith, hope, and love.

As we travel on this journey of our salvation, we are answering God's call to enter into his wild and untamable love. By his grace, we walk the ancient path, smoothed by those who have gone before us. This is the path of deep adventure. This is the way of heroic virtue.

NOTES

1. Gregory of Nyssa, *De Beatitudnibus* 1LPG 44. 1200D.

2. Peter Kreeft, *Back to Virtue: Traditional Moral Wisdom for Modern Moral Confusion* (San Francisco: Ignatius, 1992), 9.

3. Lewis Hanke, *The Spanish Struggle for Justice in the Conquest of America* (Boston: Little, Brown, 1965), 17.

4. Thomas Aquinas, *Summa Theologicae* II–II, 47, 2.

5. Bernard of Clairvaux, *De Vitis patrum* 4.42 pi73: 840d–841a.

6. Pope Benedict XVI, "Address of His Holiness Benedict XVI to the Newly Ordained Bishops" (Hall of the Swiss, Castel Gandolfo Talks, September 21, 2006).

7. St. Augustine, *Confessions*, Book 8:26

8. St. Augustine, *Confessions*, Book 8:28.

9. St. Augustine, *Confessions*, Book 10:27.

10. St. Augustine, *Letters*, 130.10(19).

11. "Letter to Proba" by St. Augustine found in the Liturgy of the Hours, Ep.130, 9, 18–10:CSEL 44, 60–63.

12. Peter Kreeft and Ronald K. Tacelli, eds., *Handbook of Christian Apologetics* (Downers Grove, IL: InterVarsity, 1994), 142.

13. Lane Cooper, ed., *The Greek Genius and Its Influence: Select Essays and Extracts* (Charleston, SC: BiblioBazaar, 2009), 271.

14. "Bl. Marianne Cope (1838–1918): Virgin, professed sister of St. Francis, missionary to leprosy patients," http://www.vatican.va/news_services/liturgy/saints/ns_lit_doc_20050514_molokai_en.html.

15. Hilde Eynikel, *Molokai: The Story of Father Damien* (Staten Island, NY: Alba, 1999), 90.

16. Hilde Van Assche-Eynikel, *Damien of Molokai* (London: Hodder and Stoughton, 1999), 324.

17. Thomas Aquinas, *Summa Theologicae* II II 23, 1.

18. St. Augustine, *Confessions*, Book 10:8.

As a World Champion surfer, ninja black belt, licensed private pilot, licensed scuba diver, and a 2015 inductee into the Sports Faith International Hall of Fame, Bear Woznick brings his sense of wonder to his DeepAdventure.Com ministries. He has pedaled his bicycle across the United States from San Diego, California, to Jacksonville, Florida. He has paddled the thirty-mile treacherous open ocean between the islands of Molokai and O'ahu. He has run with the bulls and surfed a tidal bore wave thirty kilometers up a river in Bordeaux, France. But of all of these experiences, Bear says: "The most radical thing you can do in life is abandon yourself to the wild adventure of God's will."

Bear is the author of *Deep in the Wave: A Surfing Guide to the Soul,* and is the host of the *Deep Adventure Radio* show on EWTN with millions of listeners worldwide. He is featured on EWTN'S adventure reality-show special called *Deep Adventure Quest,* and has been featured on several other TV shows including *Hawaii 5-0* and Fox's *Clean Break.*

As a graduate student at Franciscan University of Steubenville and an oblate at the Benedictine monastery in O'ahu, Bear holds Deep Adventure Quest retreats throughout the world. Spending half of his time in Cocoa Beach, Florida, and the other half in Hawaii, Bear is a sought-after speaker at conferences and retreats.

Join Bear on this quest by subscribing to his weekly audio blog at DeepAdventure.com.